JUNIOR GREAT BOOKS®

Read-Aloud Program

Teacher's Edition

Sailing Ship Series

The Great Books Foundation

A nonprofit educational organization

Copyright © 1990 by The Great Books Foundation

Chicago, Illinois

All rights reserved

ISBN 978-0-945159-74-2

13   12   11

Printed in the United States of America

Published and distributed by

The Great Books Foundation

A nonprofit educational organization

35 East Wacker Drive, Suite 400

Chicago, IL 60601

www.greatbooks.org

SFI label applies to text stock

SAILING SHIP SERIES

TEACHER'S EDITION

Welcome to the Junior Great Books® Read-Aloud program. This program will give your students continuous opportunities to interact with excellent literature and to develop their reading, writing, oral communication, and interpretive-thinking skills. The Read-Aloud program bridges the gap between children's real capacity to think interpretively about literature and their limited decoding skills—enabling all your students to think about and actively respond to high-quality literature.

Each unit in the Sailing Ship Series consists of a story or group of three poems, and a set of interpretive activities for four thirty-minute classroom sessions and an at-home session (to be completed with an adult partner). Concentrating on each selection in this way gives all children the time and the means to comprehend a rich work of literature fully, to learn from each other, and to work out their own individual perspectives.

As your class participates in the program, they will learn to communicate their ideas about the selections by exercising the whole range of language skills needed to become good readers. The children's Read-Aloud books are designed to help students practice these skills in very concrete ways—through drawing, discussing interpretive questions, and forming questions of their own. Students are also able to personalize the stories and poems through artwork and writing as they record their individual responses in their books. Throughout each unit, children can review their work in order to refresh or revise their thinking, or perhaps just to take pride in the body of work they have produced.

As in Junior Great Books for older children, you have the distinctive role of Shared Inquiry™ leader, helping students work together to find meaning in a work and to build interpretations. To fill this role, your personal curiosity about the selections, and an active interest in each child's ideas, are the best teaching equipment. As you work with the stories and poems and become familiar with the various interpretive issues in each selection, your ability to help students communicate their thoughts and develop their ideas will increase. You will also find that as you lead more Read-Aloud units, both you and your students will become more adept at exploring the issues contained in each story or group of poems.

The following introduction will give you the guidance needed to conduct the Read-Aloud program in a whole-class setting. Included are suggestions for tailoring the various activities to meet your individual classroom needs. The Read-Aloud schedule itself is meant to be flexible, and it may be adapted to suit your class size and schedule, as well as your students' skill levels. You will also find suggestions for encouraging parental involvement in the at-home portion of the program, and recommendations for recruiting parent volunteers to help out in the classroom. If you are looking for ways to integrate Read-Aloud themes into other subject areas, such as social studies, science, and math, you will find suggested topics in Appendix D.

CONTENTS

Y O U R   P R E P A R A T I O N

Prepare for the Read-Aloud program as you would normally prepare to lead Junior Great Books: read the selection through twice, taking notes as you read, and then write—ideally with a colleague—your own interpretive questions.

Since oral presentation of a literary text is central to the program, it might be a good idea to practice reading the selection aloud, so that your listeners will get the full benefit of its unique language and of your own interest and enjoyment. In particular, you may want to rehearse the poetry and those stories with a very distinctive style. However, because of the quality of the Read-Aloud selections, simply being responsive to the natural rhythm of the writing and the language itself should ensure an effective oral reading.

All of the selections in the Read-Aloud program have been carefully chosen for their emotional and imaginative appeal as well as their thematic appropriateness for young children. But it is natural that you will connect more readily with some selections than with others. Should you have difficulty connecting with a story or poem, you may want to take some additional time in your preparation to familiarize yourself with the text and to think over the interpretive issues suggested in the activities. You'll find that these selections will come alive when children offer their ideas and reactions. Sharing their curiosity and interest will richly repay your extra efforts.

Read the overview and the specific directions for each unit's activities, so that you can plan the week's schedule and anticipate any adaptations you may want to make or any materials you may need to prepare in advance. You might also want to refer to Appendix D for a list of additional readings, and for suggested ways to integrate Read-Aloud themes into other areas of your curriculum.

P R O G R A M   R O U T I N E

When you begin your Read-Aloud program, you will want to tell students some of the things that distinguish this program from their other classroom work. Let children know that each week they will be hearing a story or poem read several times, and that they will be talking about it with each other. They will be thinking about and asking a lot of different questions, including special ones called *interpretive questions.* Interpretive questions are special because they have more than one good answer.

Tell children, too, that their Read-Aloud books are special because they will get to draw in the important pictures themselves. In this way, every person's book will be unique, reflecting how each of us sees the story in our own mind. (If children wonder why the pictures in the books are in black and white, you can tell them that *they* will be supplying the color, because *their* drawings are the important ones.)

SESSION I

· Introducing the Story or Poem

We often give you a brief introduction that is meant to orient students or to provide a necessary definition or reference. For example, we suggest you prepare children for the humor of the Haitian tale "Bouki Cuts Wood" by showing them the illustration of Bouki in the tree and helping them see how easy it is to "predict" that he will fall when he cuts through the branch.

It is possible that to meet the needs of your class you will have to add to the recommended introductions. However, we suggest that you keep introductions brief, so as not to diminish the anticipation of the first reading.

· The First Reading

The first reading of a selection gives children the opportunity to experience a rich work of literature without the obstacle of difficult decoding. Listening to the unimpeded flow of a narrative, children are able to react on both an imaginative and an emotional level, and all begin their interpretive work on a selection on an equal footing. You will find that even children who can read for themselves appreciate hearing a good story or poem read aloud.

At first, you might need to experiment a little to see what type of environment is best suited for reading aloud to your class. Ideally, readings should be intimate, with children sitting in a group around you (perhaps in assigned places), so that all can clearly hear the story or poem and see the pictures.

As you read, have children listen without referring to their books. There will be opportunities for children to follow along in their books if they can during the second and third readings.

Keep interruptions during your first reading to a minimum since children will have a chance to ask questions when you are finished. Don't feel you need to define every unfamiliar word for children. Many vocabulary items add to the flavor of the work but are not crucial to understanding, and it is preferable not to break the flow of the reading.

Nor is the asking of prediction questions appropriate for this reading. Such questions lead children to speculate about what the author will specifically address—and in Shared Inquiry, children are encouraged not to guess, but to base their opinions on the text. You will want to pause and show the pictures, however, since they often depict scenes and objects that will aid children in understanding the story or poem.

· Sharing First Responses

This brief, informal exchange after the first reading of a selection allows children time to clear up any misunderstandings or factual errors. At the same time, it encourages an atmosphere in which children learn that different opinions and reactions are an important part of thinking about literature. This sharing time also allows children to see that their initial responses can provide the seeds of original ideas that are worth ongoing reflection.

After the first reading, allow five minutes or so to clear up any confusion children might have had about the story or poem. Ask them if they have any questions, and answer—or have the class answer—the factual questions. If children ask interpretive questions (which they will do naturally, especially after they have done a few units) do not engage in a lengthy discussion. Children will be far better prepared to address such questions after they have heard the selection read a few more times. Instead, tell the class that you think an interpretive question has been asked, and that they will want to think about it during the course of the week.

Children might not have any questions about the story, but they probably will have some definite reactions. Always encourage students to voice their opinions by asking them what parts of the story or poem they especially liked and why.

· The First Art Activity

The first session generally ends with an art activity, which serves as closure to the session and gives children the opportunity to record their early responses to the selection. Activities include drawing a favorite part of a story, illustrating a memorable scene or image, or expressing a reaction to a character.

Refer to the specific assignments. Occasionally, you will want to ask a few questions or have children share some ideas to help them get started on their drawings. See each unit's instruction pages for suggested questions.

AT-HOME WORK

This second reading of the selection gives children the opportunity to internalize the facts of the story or poem at a pace suited to their individual comprehension levels. In the comfortable and intimate one-on-one environment of the at-home reading, children are also able to respond more personally and thoughtfully to a selection. When discussing a story or poem at home, without the social pressures of the classroom, children feel freer to try out ideas and often do some of their most creative thinking. After students have developed some answers, and have practiced saying them out loud to another person, they are ready to continue the more formal work of the classroom with increased confidence.

When you send the Read-Aloud books home, be sure children understand what they are to do with their parents: listen as their parents read, follow along if they can, and repeat or join in saying the underlined phrases. Point out the "G.B." character and tell children that whenever they see it, they are to pause and discuss the question in the box, and circle their answer if asked to do so. Finally, they are to write or dictate their "My Question"—asking about anything in the text they wondered about—in the space provided at the end of the selection. If you feel children need a model for the kind of question to ask, think back to what they said after the first reading, formulate some questions, and write a few examples on the board. Do not feel that children's "My Questions" must be interpretive. Any question children have about the selection should be respected. Make sure students understand that the drawing assignments and the other writing assignments will be done at school. (If children are interested in G.B.'s name, tell them, or see if they can guess, that the character's initials come from the program they are participating in—*Great Books*.)

SESSION 2

· Posting "My Questions"

Displaying students' "My Questions" in a prominent place emphasizes the idea that each child's curiosity about a selection is worth considering and pursuing. Posting these questions fosters the idea of Shared Inquiry by communicating respect for each child's contribution to the group effort to understand works of literature. And as children see the questions of their classmates and point out their own questions, their reading comprehension is also bolstered.

The day after reading the selection with the at-home reader, students cut out their questions and pin them on a special Sharing Questions bulletin board. (Children who have not had an at-home reading can dictate their questions to you at this time.) Each week you might want to add the title of the unit to the bulletin board and have children decorate the board according to the unit's theme.

Tell students that they will be thinking about their questions during the next few days and discussing some of them in the Sharing Questions Discussion at the end of the week. In a few instances, a unit has no Sharing Questions Discussion, but children should still be encouraged to look at each other's questions and to listen to see if their questions are asked during the other activities.

You will want to make use of students' questions while conducting activities during the week. For instance, if a number of children ask a question that you believe is factual, you might want to address it early on. Also check to see if children's questions fall into any groupings; you may want to shape activities to pick up on their shared curiosity.

Another way to use children's questions is to cross-reference them with the textual analysis and suggested follow-up questions printed in the margins of your text, seeing if any children posed similar ones. Then, whenever possible, use the children's versions, mentioning their names. Or, introduce your question by saying that it is related to the questions asked by such and such students.

· **Reading and Review of G.B.'s Questions**

The third reading focuses on further developing students' critical-thinking skills—building on children's initial reactions to a selection as well as on the interpretations initiated during the at-home work. With the basic facts of the story or poem clear, children can concentrate on a more thoughtful, interpretive reading of the selection as they discuss important passages with their classmates. Students come to understand that reading can be both a private and a shared experience, and that meaning is enriched when ideas are pursued and explored among a community of readers.

During this reading, have students try to follow along in their books if they can, and encourage them to join in saying the underlined words and phrases. Pause when you come to G.B.'s questions and collect students' responses. Pursue their answers with appropriate follow-up questions—in effect, engage in small Shared Inquiry discussions. The questions given in the margins of your text are meant to help you develop children's thoughts about the selection. But, of course, the students' comments are the best source for your follow-up questions.

REMAINDER OF SESSION 2; SESSION 3; SESSION 4

The variety of individual and group activities created for each selection reflects the fact that young children learn and express themselves in many different ways. Because of the unhurried pacing of the units, all children have the opportunity to display their strengths and discover new ones. All activities are interpretive in nature, and thus encourage students to think more deeply about their reactions to a story or poem and to develop their own ideas about it.

Read-Aloud activities for the later sessions include dramatizations and additional art activities. At some point during Session 3 or Session 4, you will lead an interpretive discussion, either a Sharing Questions Discussion or a textual analysis. After this discussion, children will extend their experience with literature through group creative writing.

The rest of this introduction describes in detail the various Read-Aloud activities and offers guidance in how to conduct them.

INTERPRETIVE DISCUSSION

Throughout a Read-Aloud unit, children discuss their responses to the selection. But toward the end of the week, after they have expressed a variety of ideas, students are all the more prepared to build on their interpretations and come to conclusions through more formal discussion.

Sharing Questions Discussion is the culminating activity in most Read-Aloud units. It is similar to a Junior Great Books Shared Inquiry discussion, but is adapted for younger participants; it is shorter, and is based on a group of five or six interpretive questions—some of which children have contributed themselves. Your role as leader remains the same. By asking questions, you provide students with an example of a person intellectually engaged by literature.

Prepare to lead Sharing Questions Discussion by referring to the interpretive questions you wrote during your preparation and seeing if you have any to add. Then decide on the five or six questions you intend to ask your class. Note which of the children's "My Questions" are similar to the ones you plan to lead, and try to include three or four of their questions in your final list. Keep track of whose questions you use in Sharing Questions Discussion, since over the course of the semester you will want to make sure that each student has one of his or her questions mentioned at least once.

Sharing Questions Discussion will be more successful if the number of children participating is limited. Ten to fifteen children is an optimum number for discussion. A more intimate setting helps children concentrate on the questions and responses, and gives each child more opportunities to contribute ideas. If your class is large, consider dividing it into two groups. A parent volunteer can either lead one of the discussions, or conduct an activity (such as "My Favorite Words") with one group while you lead the other in discussion. Or, have one group complete an interpretive drawing assignment from the story while you lead the other group in discussion.

Begin Sharing Questions Discussion by writing your questions on the board, in the order you intend to ask them. (This practice will help children follow the discussion and focus on each question as it is being discussed.) Add children's names when appropriate. Read aloud each question in turn, and ask for answers. Through follow-up questions, explore *why* students came up with their answers. When several answers are given to an interpretive question, ask other children if they agree or disagree with what they have heard. Try to foster an exchange of opinion and to develop a few strong answers.

As in regular Shared Inquiry discussion, you will want to encourage students to give reasons for their answers by referring to the text. Children need not be able to read a passage in order to substantiate their opinions—recalling a line or a part of the text and paraphrasing it for the group is perfectly acceptable. If children are unable at first to supply textual evidence themselves, model the practice by reading aloud a passage that you think contains textual evidence for their opinions. Then ask children to explain how the passage supports their answers. In this way, students will become aware that their opinions should be based on the text, and as their reading skills develop, so will their ability to find and cite evidence on their own.

After a number of responses have been given to a question, ask children whether they have all heard an answer that satisfies them. If some students indicate that they are not yet satisfied, have them contribute additional answers at this time. Then proceed to the next question. Conclude discussion by reiterating that all the opinions offered helped everyone understand the story or poem better.

Textual analysis replaces Sharing Questions Discussion as the interpretive discussion activity in the poetry units. Textual analysis is a way for students to think about and interpret rich passages in a text. When children focus on a limited portion of the text in this way, they develop respect for the author's words and a sensitivity to their precise meanings.

Conduct a textual analysis by reading the poem or passage to the class, pausing to ask questions about lines or words that you think are worth exploring. Ask questions about what a character is thinking, about the significance of details, or about the meaning of particular phrases. Refer to the textual analysis questions printed in the margins of your text for examples of the kinds of questions to ask.

As you go through a passage, give children time to share answers and to think of their own questions if they can. Although some of your questions will have factual answers that the group can readily supply, many of your questions will be interpretive. Pursue interpretive questions with follow-up questions, just as you would in discussion.

MY FAVORITE WORDS

AN OPTIONAL ACTIVITY

At the end of each volume, pages are set aside for children to record their "favorite words"—any words in the selections that they found especially memorable. Identifying favorite words is a good way for beginning readers to increase their sight vocabularies. For children who have not yet started to read, the activity can stimulate an interest in words and introduce vocabulary work in an enjoyable way.

Explain to your class that their favorite words can—but don't have to—be new or unfamiliar ones. They can be any words or combinations of words that students find intriguing, unusual, or especially effective—for example, a word that is simply fun to say, or one that conveys a vivid picture.

If you plan to do a "My Favorite Words" activity, alert students before the second in-class reading, so they can listen for words they like. Students who are able to may underline their favorite words in the text during this second reading. After the reading, ask students for their favorite words, then write them on the board and briefly discuss the meaning of each. If appropriate, help the class consider any special features of the words that enrich their meaning, such as how they sound or what associations they have.

A class collection of favorite words could also be kept on a special, decorated Read-Aloud bulletin board, which would enable children to share and discuss their words outside of Read-Aloud time. Encourage children to keep a record of their favorite words from each selection by having them dictate or copy their words on the "My Favorite Words" page at the end of each Read-Aloud volume. Children might also want to add brief definitions on the "My Favorite Words" page. If so, they can either write, dictate, or draw a definition.

"My Favorite Words" is also a pleasant activity for children to work on at home. For example, the adult partner could help the child locate and underline favorite words during the at-home reading. The adult might also help the child record words and definitions on the "My Favorite Words" page at the end of the session.

Additional suggestions for using favorite words include asking more experienced students to select a word (or words) from their "My Favorite Words" page and compose a story or poem in which that word appears. Students might also choose a favorite word to work into a drawing. For example, children could:

Illustrate the word. Ask children to draw a picture or series of small pictures that show the word's meaning or the associations it has for the child. For example, for the word "splendor" a student might depict rays surrounding the word, or draw small pictures of such objects as a star, a sun, or a rainbow.

Make a concrete poem. Tell children that they can use the word itself (along with other words if they like) to make a picture or design. Show some examples of shaped verse, such as poems in the shape of a Christmas tree or heart, to help them get started. Encourage children to choose a shape or pattern that is appropriate to the word.

Write a hieroglyphic story or sentence. Ask children to incorporate their favorite word in a sentence or story otherwise written in pictures. Have them share and "read" each other's stories.

THE ART ACTIVITIES

Creating original art based on a reading selection is a natural and appealing way for children to connect with literature. Whenever children are asked to visualize a character or a scene through drawing, they are learning to translate the language of literature into concrete pictures. Words on a page are no longer abstractions, but become real to the child as he or she draws.

The process of visualizing some aspect of a literary work is a form of interpretation. To depict a character, for example, is to express an interpretation of that character's nature. Before drawing the lion from "Lion at School" for example, children have to pause and decide if they see the lion as mostly fierce or mostly friendly. When asked to draw the Sun from "Coyote Rides the Sun," children must determine if they think the Sun sympathizes with Coyote or wants to teach him a lesson. In other instances, children are asked to choose a scene to illustrate—for example, what they think is the funniest part of "Bouki Cuts Wood." Even this simple activity contributes to the interpretive process. For in choosing which of several possible scenes to depict, children not only visualize characters and setting, but also express the parts of the story they find most meaningful.

All of the art assignments in the Read-Aloud program are interpretive in the sense that they require the child to think about the text and to formulate a response or an opinion. Because most of the artwork is done in the student books, each child is, in effect, making a permanent record of his or her own unique vision of the story or poem. To ensure that the interpretive element is preserved in all of the art activities, the professional illustrations in the books are carefully chosen so as not to interfere with or influence the drawings the children are asked to do. The professional drawings are rendered in black and white rather than in color so that the main visual emphasis remains on the children's own artwork.

In the Read-Aloud program, the drawing assignments are designed to maximize interpretive potential. For instance, the actual drawing is usually preceded by a brief class discussion of the assignment. Having children write or dictate captions for their pictures is another way to extend their interpretive thinking. Partial captions, which children complete by adding or circling words, are included on some drawings and help bring particular interpretive issues into focus. For example, in the unit on "The Frog Went A-Traveling," the incomplete caption "The frog wants…" directs children to think about the frog's motives for leaving her comfortable swamp and setting off on a long journey south.

Especially important for promoting the concept of different, individual interpretations is the "share and compare" component of the art activities. These opportunities to share artwork can become miniature interpretive discussions in which children informally articulate their ideas and hear others' comments and insights. Depending on your preference and the arrangement of your classroom, you may try any of several ways of helping children share their art. If your children sit in small groups at tables, encourage them to explain their pictures to you and to other students in their group as you circulate during the drawing sessions. You may also have children take turns holding up their pictures before the whole class, talking about their work, and answering questions. If you have children do additional, related art projects, such as bringing in pieces of "found art" relevant to the theme of the week, these projects can be displayed in the room on a Read-Aloud bulletin board, where children can point out and discuss their contributions with other class members.

Art assignments in the Read-Aloud program are specifically tailored to each selection and represent several different types of activities. These activities include frontispieces, partially completed drawings, drawing an answer to an interpretive or evaluative question, and personal-response drawings.

Frontispieces give children an opportunity to record their early reactions to and impressions of a story. Assignments for frontispieces vary, but all are things children would be eager to do immediately after hearing the selection. Moreover, these are assignments that children can do without the interpretive insights they will acquire during subsequent readings and discussion. For example, children might be asked to respond to a specific character or incident in a story, such as illustrating the point in "The Tale of Two Bad Mice" when they like Tom Thumb and Hunca Munca most. Or, children may be asked to interpret a striking central image or scene in a story, such as drawing their interpretation of what amazing shoes the elves might have made in "The Shoemaker and the Elves."

Partially completed drawings give children the opportunity to concentrate on interpretive or evaluative issues, while providing them with a helpful context and visual stimulus. In the art activity for "The Lobster Quadrille," for example, the professional illustration of the *shingle*—a stony beach—gives children a visual idea of this new vocabulary word, while inviting them to express their own interpretation of the sea creatures' personalities as they dance the Lobster Quadrille.

Drawing an answer to an interpretive or evaluative question enables all children, whatever their level of language skill, to communicate their thinking about a selection. In the unit on "Coyote Rides the Sun," for example, children discuss four good answers to the question "Why is Coyote able to ride the Sun?" before individually choosing and illustrating the answer they consider best. In the final session on "The Frog Went A-Traveling," a discussion of the frog's character culminates in children drawing pictures supporting their individual answers to the evaluative question "Do you feel sorry for the frog at the end of the story?"

Personal-response drawings invite students to use personal experience or imaginings to create a work of art that in some way parallels or extends the text just read. For example, after reading "April Rain Song," by Langston Hughes, students draw a picture showing what *they* like to do best when it rains. To complement "Lion at School," in which a lion helps a little girl solve her problems with a class bully, children draw a picture showing where *they* would take the lion if he could be *their* friend for a day.

If time permits, you may want children to do additional drawings based on the selections, or related art projects using different media, such as collages, murals, or clay figures. Further art activity can be introduced into the program by asking children to illustrate their writing assignments or by adopting some of the suggestions discussed in the "My Favorite Words" section.

D R A M A T I Z A T I O N

Most children love acting out a story. It is a way for them to recapture the pleasure of the story and to share imaginatively in the adventures of the characters. Children's pretending also plays a special part in learning. Children often act out a new experience or idea in order to make it their own, so they can understand and use it. Dramatizations in the Read-Aloud program are designed to build on both of these aspects of pretending—joyful play and a way of thinking over something new.

In the Sailing Ship Series, children are offered a variety of dramatic activities, from dancing a "Lobster Quadrille" to acting out poems and parts of stories as you read them aloud to improvising scenes based on selections. Acting out a story or poem as it is read aloud heightens students' awareness of its details, and thus improves their grasp of the selection and their appreciation of its particular flavor and tone. When children perform Edward Lear's delightful nonsense poem "The Table and the Chair," for example, the humor of inanimate objects taking a walk becomes real for them, and they discover nuances in the poem that they might otherwise have missed.

Acting out unfamiliar situations also makes them seem more concrete and helps connect them to the rest of the plot. A dramatization is more than a plot review, however; it also helps children empathize with characters and understand relations between them. By acting out the main sequence of events in "Bouki Cuts Wood," for example, children are able to "get inside" the characters and consider how Bouki felt when he lay motionless on the ground and how the farmers felt when they thought he was dead.

Dramatizing scenes also helps children put together their ideas and build their interpretations of a selection. As they work on improvising the elves' scenes in "The Shoemaker and the Elves," for example, students can draw on their earlier responses to G.B.'s question about the elves' motives. This will prepare them to explore through their acting such interpretive questions as "Why are the elves 'puzzled' by the clothes when they first see them?" and "Why do the clothes make the elves so happy that they 'run around like wild'?" Through such dramatizations, children can experience, in an enjoyable way, the same process of thought by which an accomplished reader considers the possible meanings of parts of a story and reflects on the story as a whole. This experience is reinforced if children turn to a complementary way of expressing their interpretive insights, such as drawing, discussion, or writing.

If your class has had little experience with dramatization, you will want to set up an acting project in a fairly simple way. Most of the dramatizations in the Sailing Ship Series can be conducted with all the students acting out the entire scene or story as a group. Alternatively, different roles can be assigned to small groups of students. For example, for the dramatization of "The Table and the Chair," you might want to divide your class into Tables, Chairs, Ducks, Mice, and Beetles. For the concluding activity in the "Coyote Rides the Sun" unit, children can simply choose an appropriate animal person they would like to be and then impersonate that creature during the class's evaluative discussion of the story.

A somewhat more sophisticated way of handling dramatization is to assign a role to every child. In addition to portraying minor characters, children can play trees or wild animals of the forest, buildings or objects, and so forth, setting the scene by acting scary, friendly, welcoming, or indifferent.

Designate a stage—probably the center of the room—and place groups of actors at different stations, so they can be ready together to go "on stage." Read the story or poem aloud while children act, or read transitional parts while children fill in dialogue and action. Try to keep the action from dragging or being interrupted. As students gain confidence, encourage them to prompt each other, to suggest details, and to direct themselves.

When a class is more experienced with dramatization, you can help them reflect more on the selection while they act. Pause after especially interesting scenes to ask children how characters felt or why they acted as they did. You can also divide a more experienced class into two groups and hold back-to-back dramatizations, so that children may see and discuss differences in interpretations.

THE WRITING ACTIVITIES

Whether they write independently or "write" orally in a group, all children can benefit from composing original work. Writing extends the process of finding meaning in literature, and helps children improve their sight vocabularies. Writing about a story or poem not only stimulates interpretive thinking, it also endows those thoughts with a special importance. As an author, a child gains a sense of confidence in approaching any language-related work and develops a new way of appreciating literature.

The writing activities in the Read-Aloud program are designed to accommodate all children, whatever their inclinations or abilities. Like the art activities, the writing activities are done in the children's own books, enabling students to keep a permanent record of their thoughts about each selection.

"My Questions" are written or dictated by children after the second reading, and allow students to capture their initial curiosity about the selection. "My Questions" are first shared with the parent at the conclusion of the at-home session. They are later shared with classmates and teacher through the Sharing Questions bulletin board. It is a great source of pride for students to see their questions displayed and to hear them referred to during class discussion. If you like, the "My Question" pages can be stapled or pasted back into students' books when the unit is completed.

Captions for drawings are brief, manageable compositions that children can either dictate or write. Suitable at any stage of work on a particular text, captions give students an opportunity to clarify the interpretive content of a drawing by providing an explanation of the picture or by answering a question. Caption lines on the drawing pages often include the first few words, to focus the interpretive issue and to act as a "starter" for children's writing.

Writing an answer to a question or a reason to back up an answer gives students an opportunity to reflect on and apply their more developed understanding of the text. For example, in the "Coyote Rides the Sun" unit, children debate the question "Do you want Coyote to be chief of the animal people?" After the discussion, they are ready to circle their answers on their own and to write or dictate the main reason for their choice.

Creative-writing assignments are offered in Session 3 or Session 4 of some units and usually take the form of a group poem or song. Coming late in the week's schedule of activities, the creative-writing assignments are intended to give students an opportunity to consolidate some of their previous interpretive work in the unit and to think further about some aspect of the selection. For instance, in the unit on "The Shoemaker and the Elves," children extend their interpretations of the elves' personalities by expanding the elves' "jaunty gentlemen" song. The students add suggestions about what the elves will do now that they have fine clothes and don't have to work. Frequently, the creative-writing assignments are designed to help children develop a new perspective on a selection by drawing on their own personal experiences or imaginings. For example, after reading Robert Hillyer's "Lullaby" in the "Night into Dawn" unit, the class composes a poem about their own special real or imaginary peaceful places.

Group writing projects—with children making oral contributions as you record them on a chalkboard or chart paper—are a fun way to engage in creative writing. The whole class shares responsibility for the finished product, and children's ideas can flow freely since students themselves do not have to be concerned about the mechanics of writing.

Begin a group writing activity by explaining the object of the assignment and how you will proceed. For example, you might collect ideas from the whole class first and refine them later, or you may have each student contribute one line. If the poem has a pattern of lines or some "starters" (first lines or beginnings of lines) provided in the student books, it is helpful to copy these on the board. To help students get ideas, use questions such as those suggested in the directions for specific assignments and add others of your own. Also use questions to coax out details and more expressive language.

Sample poems are often provided to clarify directions and to assist you in thinking of questions you might ask to elicit ideas and lines from your students. The samples are not meant to be read or copied by the class. The poem structures provided are intended to give children a helpful framework for their ideas. These structures can, of course, be made shorter or longer to accommodate your class's work. Assure children that their poems need not rhyme or have a specific rhythm unless they wish them to, but do try to help them make their lines vivid and descriptive.

Writing activities in the Read-Aloud program are meant to be flexible in application, so that all students, regardless of their level of skill, can participate in the writing process and enjoy the satisfaction of seeing a written product they have helped create. If you are using the Sailing Ship Series in kindergarten or in the first semester of first grade, you will probably want to conduct all the writing assignments as whole-class oral compositions with the teacher as recorder. Second graders and more experienced first graders, on the other hand, may like to do some of the assignments individually or in small groups, perhaps after a class discussion to help them get started. In some cases, you might find it helpful to describe the assignment the day before you plan to do it in class, and let children think about, or write out, their contributions at home before pooling them in a group writing activity.

Entering group compositions in the students' books can also be adapted to suit your class's requirements. If your students do not yet write, you may transcribe their favorite lines for them. Or, you might consider providing copies of the completed projects for them to staple or paste onto the appropriate pages in their books. More experienced writers can do their own transcribing of favorite lines from the board.

For older or more experienced classes, you can easily expand the writing component of the Read-Aloud program. Students can be asked to provide captions for drawings that do not already require them, or caption ideas might be enlarged into paragraphs or stories to accompany the art assignments. Other possibilities include having students write stories or poems incorporating one or more words from their "My Favorite Words" lists, or asking them to write answers to their own "My Questions" or the interpretive questions you lead in discussion.

THE POETRY UNITS

One unit of each volume in the Sailing Ship Series consists of a group of three poems that are linked by a common theme, but are not interdependent. The structure of the poetry units is similar to that of the story units. The first poem, which is the longest or most substantial of the three, is dealt with in the first two class sessions and in the intervening at-home session. The second and third poems receive one class session apiece. However, the modular nature of the poetry units allows for flexibility in scheduling. For example, you may sometimes find it more convenient to do two poems instead of all three or to add an extra session during the week.

Aside from offering variety, working with poetry gives children an opportunity to enjoy literature that places a special emphasis on the pleasures of language—the delightful sounds of words and the compelling rhythms of lines. We stress these features by including plenty of activities that allow children to recite and act out or dance to poems. The rhymes, rhythms, and sound effects of verse enable even inexperienced readers and nonreaders to memorize and repeat selections, while the short lines and stanza breaks make it easy for children who have some reading skills to follow along for themselves. Reading poetry fosters appreciation of language for its own sake and helps stimulate children's willingness to experiment with language in their own original work. The poetry units also offer an excellent opportunity to make use of the optional "My Favorite Words" activity.

The poems, like the stories in the Read-Aloud program, are chosen for their ability to support interpretive activities, including discussion of interpretive or evaluative questions, drawing, dramatization, and group writing. Since the poems are relatively short, they can be read several times in a session. Thus, children are able to experience a feeling of real familiarity and comfort with the poems, which can translate into improved focus and concentration.

Because sound is such a vital part of poetry's appeal, you will probably want to practice reading a poem aloud a couple of times before presenting it in class. When reading aloud, let the poem's rhythm carry you, but don't change natural pronunciation to fit a set beat and don't *over*stress the accented syllables. Poets often vary even a pronounced rhythm to avoid monotony, and a metrical pattern is usually sufficiently apparent if you read in a normal tone of voice. Observe punctuation as you would with prose: if there is no punctuation at the end of a line, read right into the next line, and pause longer when a line ends with a period than when it ends with a comma. When beginning your first poetry unit, you may want to prepare children by offering a very brief introduction to the form. It should be sufficient to explain a few basic terms, such as *line* and *stanza,* and to alert them to some of the main differences between poetry and prose. Before reading any particular poem, you may wish to mention some salient feature of that selection, such as the presence or absence of rhyme or the use of an unusual rhythm.

INVOLVING PARENTS

Adult partners for the at-home portion of the Read-Aloud program fill a vital role. Confidence in and commitment to reading grow when children experience a link between the worlds of home and school. Not only does learning become easier when parents and other adults actively participate in children's efforts to understand the written word, but students also absorb the important message that reading is worthwhile.

When you describe the at-home session to parents and guardians, you will want to communicate to them their special role as reader and as a relaxed, interested listener. When asking G.B.'s questions, the adult partner or parent should keep in mind that there are no single right answers, that considering these questions is just the beginning of the child's work with the story, and that answers shouldn't be considered final. Above all, the at-home session should be fun—a cozy reading time when children and adults can share some good talk.

Appendix B provides two sample letters to send home when you initiate your Read-Aloud program. The first letter explains what the Read-Aloud program is and alerts parents and guardians to their role as adult partner in the at-home session. The second letter provides a more detailed explanation of the adult partner's responsibilities. Another very effective means of cultivating active participation is to introduce the program, by means of a short talk or visual display, at an open house or at a PTA meeting. (See Appendix C for a sample presentation highlighting the benefits of the Read-Aloud program and describing parents' at-home role.)

Recruiting volunteers to assist with the Read-Aloud program in the classroom is another way to involve parents, older students, or community members. You could ask volunteers to prepare Read-Aloud bulletin boards, to help students write captions during the art activities, or to assist you in other ways. Some programs train volunteers to lead discussions. In kindergarten and first grade, this works best when teachers are also involved. For more information on training for either teachers or volunteers, visit www.greatbooks.org and click on Professional Development.

THE SHOEMAKER AND THE ELVES

BROTHERS GRIMM
AS TOLD BY
WANDA GÁG

SESSION 1

This session consists of an introduction and first reading of the story, followed by a brief sharing of questions and comments, and an art activity in which children draw their interpretation of the beautiful shoes made by the elves.

AT-HOME WORK

During this second reading, the adult partner encourages the child to join in saying the underlined phrases, and pauses to discuss G.B.'s questions.

After reading, the adult writes the child's own question about the story into the book in preparation for the Sharing Questions Discussion (Session 3).

SESSION 2

During this reading of the story, you will collect students' responses to G.B.'s questions and lead a discussion of them. The session concludes with a dramatization of two scenes from the story—a night when the elves make shoes and the night when the elves find their new clothes.

SESSION 3

This session consists of a Sharing Questions Discussion and an art activity in which children draw their interpretation of how the shoemaker and his wife felt when they discovered the elves.

SESSION 4

This session consists of a group creative-writing activity in which children compose additional lines for the elves' song, telling what the elves will do after they become jaunty gentlemen, and an art activity in which children illustrate their favorite lines from the song.

SESSION 1

INTRODUCTION

Begin the session by telling children that this is a story about a poor shoemaker and his wife, who receive help from some elves. Explain that *elves* are small fairies.

FIRST READING AND SHARING OF RESPONSES

Ask children to listen as you read the story aloud. When you first come to the words "awl," "well-to-do," "wights," "jerkins," "jaunty," and "capers," explain them briefly, using the definitions given in the margin of your text.

After the reading, allow a few moments to clear up unfamiliar vocabulary and to let students ask questions and share their initial reactions to the story. Encourage children to offer their opinions about which parts of the story they especially liked and why.

ART ACTIVITY

Have children turn to the frontispiece, captioned "Beautiful Shoes." Tell students that they are going to imagine what kinds of amazing shoes the elves make for the shoemaker. Let children know that they can draw one pair or many pairs. Allow time for students to share and compare their drawings.

SESSION 2

POSTING "MY QUESTIONS"

Have students cut out the questions they wrote at home and pin them on the Sharing Questions bulletin board. Children who have not had an at-home reading can dictate their questions to you at this time. Encourage children to look at the Sharing Questions bulletin board during the week, to point out their own questions and to ask about those of their classmates.

READING AND REVIEW OF G.B.'S QUESTIONS

Read the story aloud, encouraging children to follow along in their books if they can. Pause to collect students' responses to G.B.'s questions (pages 9, 11, and 17). Help students think further about their responses by asking follow-up questions such as those given in the margin of your text.

SESSION 2 (continued)

DRAMATIZATION

Tell students that they are going to pretend to be the elves on two different nights. First, they will act out a night when the elves go to the shoemaker's workroom to make shoes. Then they will act out the night when the elves go to the workroom and find their new clothes.

Set the first scene by helping students think about what the workroom would look like and by reminding them that the elves slip in quietly at night and work very quickly. After a brief discussion of such questions as *How do you think the elves would act?* and *What do you think the elves would say to each other?*, have students improvise the scene. If the class wishes to include dialogue, help them get started by reminding them of their responses to G.B.'s first question.

After students have completed the first scene, tell them that the elves are going to come into the workroom again, and that *this time* they will discover the clothes. Have students discuss for a moment or two how the elves will react. You may want to remind children that in the story the elves were puzzled by the clothes before they put them on and realized they were "'jaunty gentlemen." Students might conclude the second improvisation by joining hands in a dance.

SESSION 3

SHARING QUESTIONS DISCUSSION

Prepare for discussion as usual, deciding on the five or six interpretive questions you intend to ask the class. Note which of the children's questions are similar to those you plan to lead and try to include three or four of their questions in your final list. When you write your questions on the board, include children's names as appropriate.

Suggested Interpretive Questions

Why isn't the shoemaker worried when he only has enough leather left for one pair of shoes? Why does he go to bed "peacefully"?

Why is it the shoemaker's wife, and not the shoemaker himself, who suggests thanking the elves by making clothes for them?

Why are the elves "puzzled" by the clothes when they first see them?

Why do the clothes make the elves so happy that they "run around like wild"?

Why do the shoemaker and his wife continue to have good luck even after the elves go away?

SESSION 3 (continued)

ART ACTIVITY

Have students turn to the page captioned "The shoemaker and his wife feel...." Remind children that the shoemaker and his wife hid in the workroom one night in order to find out who was making the shoes for them. Tell students that they are going to draw a picture showing the shoemaker and his wife when they discover the pretty little elves. To help children get started, ask such questions as *How do you think the shoemaker and his wife felt when they saw the elves? Were they surprised? Frightened? Amused? Grateful? Relieved? Why don't the shoemaker and his wife speak to the elves?*

As students draw, circulate among them and help them complete their captions. Allow time for students to share and compare their drawings.

SESSION 4

GROUP CREATIVE WRITING AND ART ACTIVITY

Write on the board or chart paper the title "Elf Song" and the lines "Now we are jaunty gentlemen,/Why should we ever work again?" Read the lines aloud and tell students that together they are going to add some more lines to the song, describing what the elves will do now that they have fine clothes and do not have to work.

Allow a few moments for students to think about their ideas. Then ask them to share their thoughts about what the elves will do. Record students' ideas on the blackboard or chart paper, beginning each line with the words "Now we will...."

When the song is completed, read it back to the class. Make copies for students to paste into their books on the page titled "Elf Song," or help children copy their favorite line in the space provided. Students can then illustrate their favorite line on the page captioned "What the Elves Will Do."

Allow time for students to share and compare their drawings.

THE SHOEMAKER AND THE ELVES

BROTHERS GRIMM

Beautiful Shoes

There was once a shoemaker who made shoes and made them well. Yet luck was against him for, although he worked hard every day, he became poorer and poorer until he had nothing left but enough leather for one pair of shoes.

That evening he cut out the leather for the last pair of shoes, and then after laying the pieces in a neat row on his workbench, he said his prayers and went peacefully to bed.

"I'll get up early in the morning,"
he thought. "Then I can finish the shoes
and perhaps sell them."

But when he arose the next morning,
the pieces of cut leather were nowhere
to be seen, and in their stead stood
a pair of beautiful shoes, all finished
to the last seam, and sewn so neatly, too,
that there was not a flaw nor a false
stitch in them. The shoemaker was amazed
and did not know what to make of
it, but he picked up the shoes and set
them out for sale. Soon a man came and
bought them, and because he was so
pleased with their fine workmanship, he
paid more than the usual price for
them. With this money the shoemaker
was able to buy enough leather for
two pairs of shoes.

As before, he cut the leather for
the next day's sewing, laid it out on his
workbench and went to bed. In the morning,

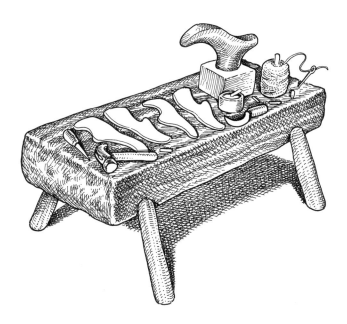

there again were the shoes—two pairs
this time—all ready to wear. The hammer,
the knife, the awl, the wax and twine,
the needles and pegs, still lay about on the
bench as though someone had been
working there, yet no one could be seen.
The shoemaker didn't know how such
a thing could happen but he was glad it
happened, all the same. Again he was lucky
enough to sell the shoes for more
than the usual price, and this time he
was able to buy enough leather for
four pairs of shoes.

awl: a tool for
making holes in
leather

Do you like making shoes?

*Are you pleased with the
shoes you make?*

*Why did you wait until the
shoemaker had only enough
leather for one pair of
shoes to help him?*

*Do you feel sorry for the
shoemaker?*

Imagine you are
one of the elves.
Why are you helping
the shoemaker?

9

Well, so it went on. Night after night he cut out the leather and laid it on his workbench; morning after morning, there stood a row of handsome shoes, ready to sell, ready to wear. And day after day buyers came and paid such a good price for the shoes that the shoemaker was able to buy more and more leather, and sell more and more shoes until at last he was poor no longer and even became a well-to-do man.

well-to-do: rich

Then one evening—it was not long
before Christmas—the shoemaker,
after laying out the leather for many pairs
of shoes, went to his wife and said,
"How would it be now, if we stayed awake
tonight and watched for a while?
I would like to see who it is, or what
it can be, that is so good to us."

Why does the
shoemaker wait
until he is rich
to find out who
is helping him?

*Why does the
shoemaker want
to see who is
helping him?*

*Why wasn't the
shoemaker curious
to find out who
was making the
shoes earlier?*

"Yes," said his wife, "that I would like to know too."

They lit a candle and set it on the table, then hid in a corner behind some clothes which were hanging there.  Here they waited until at last, just at midnight, there came two pretty little elves without a stitch of clothing to cover them. Quickly the little creatures sprang upon the workbench and began making shoes. Swiftly and nimbly they worked—piercing and punching and sewing, pegging and pounding away with such skill that the man and his wife could scarcely believe their eyes.

And so the little elves worked on with tiny flying fingers, and didn't stop for a moment until all the shoes were finished down to the last stitch and peg.

The shoemaker and his wife feel _____

_____

Then, in a twinkling, they leaped up
and ran away. Next morning the woman
said, "Husband, what I was going to say,
those little elves have made us so rich—to
show our thanks would be no more than
right. There they run around, poor little

wights: creatures

wights, all bare and must surely freeze.
Do you know what? I will make them
some clothes and knit them each a pair
of stockings. You can make them each
a pair of little shoes, yes?"

Oh yes, the shoemaker would gladly do that. And so one evening, when everything was ready, they laid out their presents instead of the cut-out leather, then hid once more behind the clothes in the corner and waited to see what the little creatures would do.

At midnight, there came the two little elves, skipping along, ready to sit down and work as usual. They looked, but saw no leather anywhere. They looked again and spied the row of little garments lying on the workbench: two little shirts and jerkins, two pairs of breeches, two peaked hats, four little stockings and four tiny shoes with pointed toes. At first they

jerkins: sleeveless jackets

15

seemed puzzled, as though wondering what these things were for, but then, when they understood that the clothes were meant for them, they were filled with joy. Quickly they picked up one little garment after another, dressing themselves with lightning speed; and all the time they laughed with delight, and sang:

jaunty: lively

> **"Now we are jaunty gentlemen,**
> **Why should we ever work again?"**

When they were fully dressed, from peaky hats to pointed shoes, they began to skip and run around like wild, so glad and gleeful were they. There seemed

capers: lively leaps

to be no end to their capers as they leaped over the chairs, and delved among the shelves and benches, but at last,

16

after spinning round and round like tiny tops, they clasped hands and went dancing out of the door.

They never came back, but the shoemaker and his wife were always lucky after that, and they never forgot the two little elves who had helped them in their time of need.

Why do the elves never return after they get their shoes and clothing?

Why are the elves so glad and gleeful after they get their clothes?

Why hadn't the elves ever made shoes and clothes for themselves?

Why do the elves think that they no longer have to work once they have their new clothes?

17

Elf Song

Now we are jaunty gentlemen,

Why should we ever work again?

Now we will _____

_____

What the Elves Will Do

My Question

_____

_____

Name _____

THE FROG WENT A-TRAVELING

RUSSIAN FOLKTALE
AS TOLD BY
VSEVOLOD GARSHIN

SESSION 1

This session consists of an introduction and first reading of the story, followed by a brief sharing of questions and comments, and an art activity in which children draw the frog when she is flying with the ducks.

AT-HOME WORK

During this second reading, the adult partner encourages the child to join in saying the underlined words and phrases, and pauses to discuss G.B.'s three questions. Children respond to the third question by circling their answer.

After reading, the adult writes the child's own question about the story into the book in preparation for the Sharing Questions Discussion (Session 3).

SESSION 2

During this reading of the story, you will collect students' responses to G.B.'s questions and lead a discussion of them. The session concludes with an art activity in which students draw their interpretation of what kind of life the frog hopes to find when she leaves her home.

SESSION 3

This session consists of a Sharing Questions Discussion and an art activity in which children draw a real or imaginary place they would like to visit.

SESSION 4

This session consists of an evaluative discussion in which children consider whether or not they feel sorry for the frog, and an art activity in which children draw a picture showing why they do or do not feel sorry for the frog.

SESSION 1

INTRODUCTION

Begin the session by telling children that this is a Russian folktale about a frog who goes on an unusual journey. Explain that frogs like to eat insects and often live in *swamps,* areas of land that are partly covered by water.

FIRST READING AND SHARING OF RESPONSES

Ask children to listen as you read the story aloud. When you first come to the words "undignified," "enchanted," and "cleverness," explain them briefly, using the definitions given in the margin of your text.

After the reading, allow a few moments to clear up unfamiliar vocabulary and to let students ask questions and share their initial reactions to the story. Encourage children to offer their opinions about which parts of the story they especially liked and why.

ART ACTIVITY

Have children turn to the frontispiece, captioned "Travel by Ducks." Tell them that they are going to draw a picture of the frog when she flies by hanging on a stick carried by the ducks. Help students get started by re-reading the frog's description of her idea for flying on page 33 beginning, "I thought of something!" and ending, "all will go well."

Allow time for students to share and compare their drawings.

SESSION 2

POSTING "MY QUESTIONS"

Have students cut out the questions they wrote at home and pin them on the Sharing Questions bulletin board. Children who have not had an at-home reading can dictate their questions to you at this time. Encourage children to look at the Sharing Questions bulletin board during the week, to point out their own questions and to ask about those of their classmates.

READING AND REVIEW OF G.B.'S QUESTIONS

Read the story aloud, encouraging children to follow along in their books if they can. Pause to collect students' responses to G.B.'s questions (pages 30, 35, and 40). Help students think further about their responses by asking follow-up questions such as those given in the margin of your text.

SESSION 2 (continued)

ART ACTIVITY

Have students turn to the page captioned "The frog wants...." Tell them that they are going to draw a picture showing what kind of life they think the frog hopes to find when she leaves her swamp home and goes with the ducks. To help children get ideas, ask such questions as *What do you think the frog wants that she hasn't got at the beginning of the story? More food? Freedom? Adventure? New friends? What things in life are most important to her?*

As children draw, circulate among them and help them complete their captions. Allow time for students to share and compare their drawings.

SESSION 3

SHARING QUESTIONS DISCUSSION

Prepare for discussion as usual, deciding on the five or six interpretive questions you intend to ask the class. Note which of the children's questions are similar to those you plan to lead and try to include three or four of their questions in your final list. When you write your questions on the board, include children's names as appropriate.

Suggested Interpretive Questions

Why does the frog worry about being "undignified" when she is in her own swamp?

Why does the frog lie to the ducks about why she wants to fly closer to the ground?

*Why does the frog want the villagers to know that **she** is the one who figured out a way for her to fly? Why does this finally make her lose all self-control?*

Why is "I did! I thought of it!" the first thing the frog says after almost being killed falling into the pond?

Why do the ducks just assume the frog is dead? Why don't they fly down and find out?

SESSION 3 (continued)

ART ACTIVITY

Have children turn to the page captioned "A Place I Would Like to Visit." Remind them that the frog was happy in her swamp, but when she heard the ducks talk about the south, she decided she wanted to go there.

Tell students that they are going to draw a picture of a real or imaginary place *they* would like to visit. Help them get started by asking them to think about whether they would choose a warm or a cold place, the city or the country, someplace they have seen before, or someplace completely new and different. Ask such questions as *What would you see and do in this place? Why would you want to go to this place?*

Allow time for children to share and compare their drawings.

SESSION 4

EVALUATIVE DISCUSSION

Write on the board or chart paper the following question and answers:

Do you feel sorry for the frog at the end of the story?

Yes   No

Read the question aloud and ask students for their answers. Have them give reasons for their opinions, supported by the story. At the conclusion of your discussion, summarize some of the main reasons given to support each answer.

ART ACTIVITY

When students have completed the evaluative discussion, ask them to turn to the page captioned "I do/do not feel sorry for the frog because...." Tell students that they are going to draw a picture of something the frog does, or something that happens to her, that explains why they do or do not feel sorry for her.

As children draw, circulate among them and help them circle "do" or "do not" and complete their captions. Allow time for children to share and compare their drawings.

THE FROG
WENT
A-TRAVELING

RUSSIAN FOLKTALE

Travel by Ducks

Once upon a time there lived a frog.
She inhabited a swamp, went after
mosquitoes and other tiny creatures,
and in the spring she croaked loudly
together with her frog friends. And this
is the way she would have peacefully
lived on and on if, of course, a stork
did not gobble her up in the meantime.
But something unusual happened.

One day she was sitting on a knot of
a tree stump that jutted out of the water,
enjoying a warm drizzle.

"My, what lovely wet weather we're having today!" she thought. "What a delight it is to be alive in this fine world!"

The drizzle fell gently on the frog's shiny little back, the drops ran down her tummy and her fat little legs and this was wonderfully pleasant, so pleasant that she almost croaked. But, fortunately, she remembered that it was already fall and that in the fall frogs did not croak—this was done only in the spring. To croak in the wrong season of the year would be most undignified. So she kept quiet and continued to enjoy herself.

Suddenly the frog heard a thin whistling sound. There is a certain breed of ducks who make this kind of sound when they are in flight. As their wings cut

undignified: not the right or proper way to behave

26

the air they make the sound of a whistled song. Few-few-few-few, one hears as a flock of these ducks soars high in the sky— they fly so high that you can't even see them. This time, flying in a semicircle, the ducks came down and sat in the very same swamp where the frog made her home.

"**Quack-quack!**" one of them said. "We still have far to go. We had better stop and eat."

The frog hid herself at once.
She knew that the ducks would not make
a meal out of her, for she was too large
and too fat for that; but to be quite safe,
she dived under the tree stump. But, after
giving the matter a little more thought,
she decided to raise her head out of the
water and watch the ducks. She was
very curious to know where the ducks
were going.

"**Quack-quack!**" another duck said.
"**Br-r-r-r, it's getting cold!** Let's hurry south!
Let's hurry south!"

And all the other ducks quacked in
agreement.

"Pardon me, ladies and gentlemen
ducks," the frog made bold to say,

"but what is this south to which
you are flying? Please forgive me for this
interruption."

The ducks surrounded the frog.
At first they felt like eating her up,
but each duck decided that the frog was
too big and would stick in the throat.
Then they began to quack loudly,
flapping their wings.

"It's good in the south! It's warm
there now. There are such warm swamps!
And what worms! It's perfectly lovely
in the south!"

They quacked so loudly that the
frog thought she'd get deaf from it.
When she finally got them to quiet down,
she asked one of them, a duck who was
fatter than the others and seemed
more wise, what was "south." And when
the frog heard all about it she was
enchanted, but asked just the same,
because she was a careful frog:

enchanted:
delighted, fascinated

29

"But are there many mosquitoes and other insects there?"

"Oh, clouds of them!" the wise fat duck answered.

"Croak!" the frog croaked and looked around at once to make sure that none of the other frogs heard her do this out of season. She just couldn't resist croaking at least once.

"Take me with you!" she said to the ducks.

Why does the frog want to leave her pleasant swamp and fly south with the ducks?

Why is the frog's curiosity stronger than her need to feel safe from the ducks?

Why do the ducks become so excited when they tell the frog about the south?

Why can't the frog resist croaking at least once when the ducks tell her about the south?

The frog wants _____

"You surprise me!" exclaimed the wise fat duck. "How can we take you with us? You have no wings."

"When are you starting out again?" the frog asked.

"Soon, soon!" the ducks screamed. **"Quack-quack! Quack-quack!** It's cold here! To the south! To the south!"

"Allow me to think for just five minutes," said the frog. "I'll be back very soon. I'm sure I can think of something."

The frog leaped into the water from the stump onto which she had climbed again, and dived to the bottom of the

swamp, there to think undisturbed.
Five minutes passed and the ducks were
about to fly off, when the frog
appeared again. Her face was beaming
as only a frog's face can beam.

"I thought of something! I have
an idea!" she announced. "Let two of you
hold the end of a twig in your beaks;
I'll hang on to it in the middle with my
mouth. You'll fly and I'll ride. If you
don't quack and I don't croak, all
will go well."

The ducks saw little pleasure in
dragging a heavy frog for three thousand
miles in complete silence, but they were
so impressed with the frog's cleverness
that they all agreed to take her along.

cleverness: intelligence

They decided to take turns and change
conductors every two hours. And since
there were ducks in this flock almost
without count, and only one frog to
transport, it wasn't going to be too much
work for any single duck.

So they found a strong twig, two of
the ducks raised it in their beaks, the frog
leaped up and grabbed the middle of it
with her mouth, and off they went.
The frog almost lost her breath from fright
as they flew higher and higher, especially
since the ducks didn't fly smoothly
and jerked the twig. The poor frog swayed
in the air like a clown on a trapeze.
She clamped the twig as tightly as she
could in her jaw so as not to lose
hold of it and be hurled to the ground.
However, she soon got used to it
all and even began to look around.
Fields, meadows, rivers, and mountains

sped by under her. It was hard for her to get a good look at these places because she was facing forward. But she managed to see some of the landscape, and was happy and proud that she was taking such an unusual journey.

"That was pretty clever of me," she thought.

And the other ducks followed the pair in front who were carrying the frog, and they screamed and praised her.

"What a clever one is our frog!" they said. "There are few who are that clever even among us ducks."

Why does the frog's cleverness make the ducks decide to take the trouble of carrying her south?

Why do the ducks praise the frog and say that she is even more clever than most ducks?

Why are the ducks so proud of the frog's cleverness?

Why do the ducks call her "our" frog?

The frog could barely resist thanking them, but remembering that if she opened her mouth to speak she would drop from the terrible height, she held on to the twig even more tightly and decided to be patient and silent.

All day long the frog hung on this way. The ducks took turns carrying her, changing drivers in mid-air. This was very scary for the frog, and she nearly screamed with fright several times.

In the evening they would stop for a rest in some swamp and at dawn they would continue their journey. After the first day the frog rode facing backward in order to see better the places they flew over. They passed harvested fields, golden forests, and meadows full of haystacks. From the villages they could hear the sound of people's voices and the noise of threshing.

The peasants looked up at the flock of ducks and, noticing that they were carrying something, pointed and made some remarks. The frog wished they were flying nearer to the ground so that she could show off and hear what the villagers were saying about her. Next time they stopped for a rest she said:

"Couldn't we fly a little lower? I get so dizzy from flying so high, and I'm afraid that I'll fall if I get sick to my stomach."

And the kind ducks promised that they would fly lower. Next day they flew so low that they could hear every word the villagers were saying.

"Look, look!" some peasant children cried in one village, "the ducks are carrying a frog."

The frog heard this and her heart leaped with pride.

"Look, look!" some grown-ups cried in another village. "What a miracle!"

"I wonder if they realize that it was *I* who thought of it and not the ducks," the frog thought.

"Look, look!" the people cried in a third village. "What a sight! Who could have thought of such a clever trick?!"

The frog now lost all self-control and, forgetting to be careful, cried with all her might:

"I did! I did!"

And saying this she lost hold of the twig and somersaulted down toward the earth. The ducks yelled loudly. One of them tried to catch the falling frog in mid-air, but missed. The frog

was coming down fast. Luckily she
fell into a muddy pond on the edge
of the village.

The frog quickly came up to the
surface and again screamed as loudly as
she could:

"I did! I thought of it!"

But there was no one there to
hear her. Frightened by the sudden splash
when the frog fell into the water, the other
frogs hid beneath it. When they came up
again they stared at the newcomer,
wondering who she was.

And the frog told them the amazing
story of how all her life she tried to
think of a new way of traveling and how
she at last invented "travel by ducks."
She told them that she had her own
ducks who carried her wherever and
whenever she wished to go and that
she had traveled this way to the south
where it was very pleasant and where
there were wonderful warm swamps
and lots of insects of all kinds.

"I came here to see how *you* live,"
she added. "I think I might stay with
you until the spring, when my ducks—
to whom I gave a vacation—will return."

But, of course, the ducks never came
back. They thought that the frog had
been killed in the fall, and they felt
very sorry for her.

Why does the frog
tell some lies in
her story about
how she came to
the pond?
(Circle your
favorite answer.)

1. She wants to
   show off.

2. She believes the
   lies are the truth.

3. She is embarrassed.

4. Other _____
   _____
   _____

*Why does the frog say she
had tried all her life to think
of a new way of traveling,
when she really invented
"travel by ducks" in five
minutes?*

*Why does she tell the other
frogs, "I came here to see
how you live"?*

*Does the frog really believe
that "her" ducks will return
for her?*

*Why does the frog boast
about her life to the other
frogs and present herself
as being so special?*

A Place I Would Like to Visit

I ^do^
 ~do not~ feel sorry for the frog because _____

_____

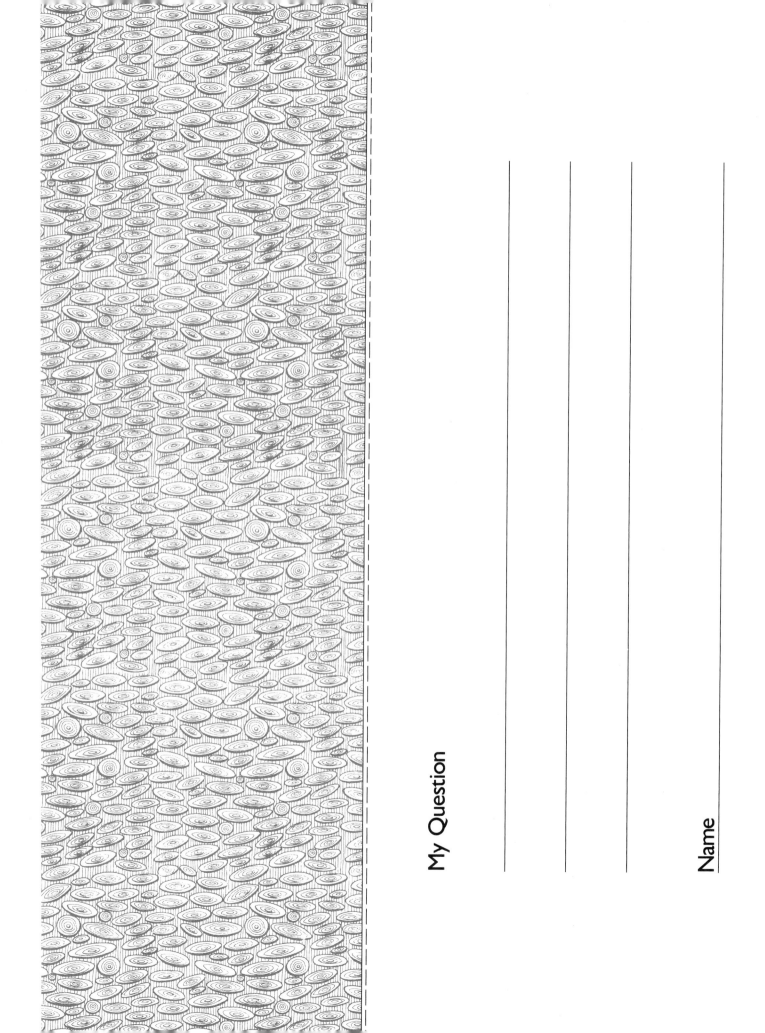

My Question

Name

NIGHT INTO DAWN

POETRY BY

ROBERT HILLYER

AND

JOHN CIARDI,

AND A

MESCALERO APACHE SONG

SESSION 1: "Lullaby"

This session consists of an introduction, two readings of the poem, and an art activity in which children draw their interpretation of the shadowy shore.

If possible, bring to class a piece of velvet, preferably a dark color, to help children grasp the image of "velvet things" in the poem.

AT-HOME WORK: "Lullaby"

The adult partner reads the poem through once, encouraging the child to join in saying the underlined words and phrases. The adult then reads the poem a second time, pausing to discuss G.B.'s three questions. Children respond to the third question by circling their answer.

After reading, the adult writes the child's own question about "Lullaby" into the book.

SESSION 2: "Lullaby"

During this reading of the poem, you will collect students' responses to G.B.'s questions and lead a discussion of them. The session concludes with a group creative-writing activity in which children compose a poem about their favorite real or imaginary peaceful places, and an art activity in which they draw a picture of their favorite peaceful place.

SESSION 3: "What Night Would It Be?"

This session consists of an introduction and first reading of the poem, a second reading and discussion of the poem, and a writing and art activity in which children compose and illustrate a "riddle" poem about a holiday or special celebration.

SESSION 4: "Dawn Song"

This session consists of an introduction and first reading of the poem, a second reading with textual analysis, and an art activity in which children create a mural showing their interpretations of the images in the poem. See the Session 4 activities page for the necessary art materials.

SESSION 1: "Lullaby"

INTRODUCTION

Introduce the poem by telling children that it is a *lullaby,* a poem or song to listen to before you go to sleep.

FIRST AND SECOND READINGS

Ask children to listen as you read the poem aloud. Before reading the poem a second time, take a few moments to let children ask questions and make comments. Also help children clear up such unfamiliar vocabulary as "wake," "blade," "brakes," "prow," and "rushes," using the definitions given in the margin of your text.

Read the poem aloud a second time, encouraging students to follow along in their books if they can, and to join in saying the underlined words and phrases. Students might enjoy imitating the motion of paddling a canoe while they repeat the underlined words.

ART ACTIVITY

Have students turn to the frontispiece, captioned "The Shadowy Shore." Tell them that they are going to draw a picture showing what they think the shadowy shore would look like. To help students get further into the mood of the poem, have them close their eyes and imagine what it would be like to walk along the shadowy shore when everyone else is asleep. Ask such questions as *Are you on a rocky shore or a sandy beach? What do you see? Are there any birds or animals awake? Can you see the moon or the stars? What colors can you see around you?* Tell students that they can include the canoe and the lake in their pictures if they like. Allow time for them to share and compare their drawings.

SESSION 2: "Lullaby"

POSTING "MY QUESTIONS"

Have students cut out the questions they wrote at home. Glance through them briefly and note any that you might want to raise during your discussion of G.B.'s questions. Then pin students' questions on the Sharing Questions bulletin board. Let children know that even though there will be no Sharing Questions Discussion this week, they should still look at the bulletin board and talk about their questions with each other.

READING AND REVIEW OF G.B.'S QUESTIONS

Read the poem aloud, pausing to collect students' responses to G.B.'s questions. Ask children to give reasons for their answers, and then help them think further about the poem by asking additional questions such as those given in the margin of your text.

GROUP CREATIVE WRITING

Tell children that they are going to write a poem about real or imaginary places that they think would be especially pleasant and peaceful. Write on the board or a piece of chart paper the poem's title and the outline of the first stanza, as follows:

Peaceful Places

It is peaceful _____

Because _____

SESSION 2: "Lullaby" (continued)

Explain to students that they will say where their peaceful place is in the first line and describe what makes this place especially nice and peaceful in the second line. As children offer their examples, help them develop their ideas into more descriptive second lines by asking such questions as *What does your peaceful place look like? What sounds or colors do you find there? Why is this place especially peaceful?* Continue adding stanzas following the two-line pattern above until all children who wish to contribute have done so.

When the poem is finished, read it back to the class. Make copies for students to paste into their books on the page titled "Peaceful Places," or help them copy their favorite stanzas on the lines provided.

Here is a brief example of a poem that a class might compose:

Peaceful Places

It is peaceful on top of a cloud
Because it is soft and silent and high above the ground.

It is peaceful in my backyard
Because I can hear the birds sing and the bees buzz.

It is peaceful in my bed at night
Because it is warm and cozy and no one is talking.

ART ACTIVITY

Have children turn to the page captioned "My Peaceful Place." Ask them to illustrate their favorite lines from their poem, or to draw another favorite peaceful place of their own.

SESSION 3: "What Night Would It Be?"

INTRODUCTION

Introduce the poem by telling students that it is a kind of riddle—a poem that describes something but doesn't tell what it is until the end. Ask them to listen carefully for the clues in the poem.

FIRST READING

Ask children to listen as you read the poem aloud. Afterward, take a few moments to let children ask questions and make comments, and clear up unfamiliar vocabulary.

SECOND READING AND DISCUSSION

Read the poem through a second time, encouraging students to follow along in their books if they can, and to join in saying the underlined phrases. Then help students briefly discuss the poem by asking such questions as *What are some of the scary things in the poem? What are some of the fun things in the poem? Why is it sometimes fun to be scared?*

GROUP CREATIVE WRITING AND ART ACTIVITY

Tell students that they are going to write their own "riddle" poem about a holiday or special celebration. Write on the board or a piece of chart paper the title "What Day Would It Be?" and copy the outline of the poem, given in the student book.

SESSION 3: "What Night Would It Be" (continued)

Have students choose a special day, such as a holiday or a birthday, and fill in the name of the day on the final line of the poem. Then ask the class to think of things that help to make that day special—for example, particular foods, decorations, clothing, and activities. Use students' suggestions to create the first stanza of the poem.

When the poem is finished, read it back to the class. Make copies for students to paste into their books on the page titled "What Day Would It Be?" or help them copy their favorite lines in the space provided. If time allows, children can use the remaining space on the page to illustrate their favorite lines.

Here is a brief example of a poem that a class might compose:

What Day Would It Be?

If there are hot dogs and lemonade,
Red, white, and blue banners,
Parades and picnics,
Brass bands and baseball,
And fireworks in the sky,

What day would it be?
It must be the Fourth of July!

SESSION 4: "Dawn Song"

INTRODUCTION

Introduce the poem by telling children that it is a Mescalero Apache song to celebrate the *dawn*, or sunrise. Explain that the Apache are a Native American people living in the southwestern United States, and that the Mescalero are a tribe of the Apache nation.

FIRST READING

Have children listen while you read the poem through once. Then take a few moments to let children ask questions and make comments, and clear up unfamiliar vocabulary.

SECOND READING AND TEXTUAL ANALYSIS

Read the poem aloud a second time, encouraging students to follow along in their books if they can, and to join in saying the underlined phrases. During the second reading, pause to conduct a textual analysis, using questions such as those printed in your text.

ART ACTIVITY

For this activity, you will need to supply mural paper and crayons, paints, or markers. Explain to students that they are going to make a mural illustrating the different ways the dawn is described in the poem. Briefly review the images mentioned in the poem, such as the sunbeams fanning out like feathers from a black turkey's tail, the boys with sunshine shoes, the dawn maidens in yellow shirts dancing from the rainbow, and the green and yellow mountains. You may want to help students get started by sketching in the outline of the mountains on the mural paper ahead of time. Have students choose their favorite images to draw on the mural.

NIGHT INTO DAWN

POETRY

The Shadowy Shore

LULLABY

The long canoe
Toward the shadowy shore,
One…two…
Three…four…
The paddle dips,
Turns in the wake,
Pauses, then
Forward again,
Water drips
From the blade to the lake.

wake: trail a boat
makes in the water

blade: flat, wide
part of a paddle

Why would being in
the long canoe
make you sleepy?

Why is it restful to
be on or near
water?

What is peaceful
about the way the
canoe moves
through the water?

47

Nothing but that,
No sound of wings;
The owl and bat
Are velvet things.
No wind awakes,
No fishes leap,
No rabbits creep
Among the brakes.

brakes: thick
bushes

Why are the owl
and the bat called
"velvet things"?

How does velvet
look and feel?

How does night
make things like
velvet?

Why would
something velvet
be very quiet?

The long canoe
At the shadowy shore,
One…two…
Three…four…
A murmur now
Under the prow
Where rushes bow
To let us through.
One…two…
Upon the shore,
Three…four…
Upon the lake,
No one's awake,
No one's awake,
One…
Two…
No one,
Not even
You.

—Robert Hillyer

prow: the front of a boat

rushes: grasslike plants that grow in or near water

What would you like most about being on the peaceful lake? (Circle one.)

1. The coziness inside the canoe.

2. The smooth movement of the canoe as it glides through the water.

3. The gentle sounds of the water.

4. Other _____ _____ _____

What makes the canoe cozy?

How does gliding through the water in a canoe make you feel?

Why do the gentle sounds of the water make you feel sleepy?

49

Peaceful Places

It is peaceful _____

Because _____

It is peaceful _____

Because _____

My Peaceful Place

My Question

_____

_____

_____

Name _____

WHAT NIGHT WOULD IT BE?

If the moon shines

On the black pines

And an owl flies

And a ghost cries

And the hairs rise

On the back

   on the back

      on the back of your neck—

If you look quick

At the moon-slick

On the black air

And what goes there

Rides a broom-stick

And if things pick

At the back

at the back

at the back of your neck—

Would you know then

By the small men

With the lit grins

And with no chins,

By the owl's *hoo,*

and the ghost's *boo,*

By the Tom Cat,

And the Black Bat,

On the night air,

And the thing there,

By the thing,

   by the thing,

      by the dark thing there

(Yes, you do,
yes, you do
know the thing I mean)

That it's now,
   that it's now,
      that it's…Halloween!

—John Ciardi

What Day Would It Be?

If there are _____

_____

_____

What day would it be?

It must be _____

DAWN SONG

Textual Analysis Questions

How does the dawn look like the beautiful tail of a turkey?

What would yellow shoes of sunbeams be like? How would it feel to wear them?

The black turkey in the east spreads his tail
The tips of his beautiful tail are the white dawn

Boys are sent running to us from the dawn
They wear yellow shoes of sunbeams

They dance on streams of sunbeams

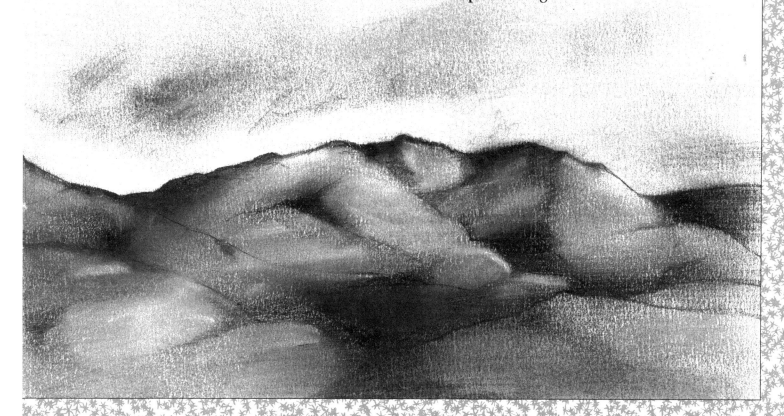

Textual Analysis Questions

What do you think the girls from the rainbow would look like? Why do they dance?

Why do the mountains turn to green and yellow at dawn?

Girls are sent dancing to us from the rainbow
They wear shirts of yellow

They dance above us the dawn maidens

The sides of the mountains turn to green
The tops of the mountains turn to yellow

And now above us on the beautiful mountains
 it is dawn.

—Mescalero Apache song

THE TALE OF TWO BAD MICE

BEATRIX POTTER

OVERVIEW

SESSION 1

This session consists of an introduction and first reading of the story, followed by a brief sharing of questions and comments, and an art activity in which children draw the part of the story where they like the two bad mice the most.

AT-HOME WORK

During this second reading, the adult partner pauses to discuss G.B.'s three questions. Children respond to the first question by circling their answer.

After reading, the adult writes the child's own question about the story into the book in preparation for the Sharing Questions Discussion (Session 4).

SESSION 2

During this reading of the story, you will collect students' responses to G.B.'s questions and lead a discussion of them. The session concludes with an art activity in which students draw a picture of what they think Hunca Munca might have brought back from the doll's-house.

SESSION 3

This session consists of an art activity in which children depict a time in their lives when they felt disappointed and angry, like the two mice, and a dramatization in which children act out the end of the story.

SESSION 4

This session consists of a Sharing Questions Discussion and an art activity in which children draw their interpretation of the effect the policeman doll has upon the two mice.

SESSION 1

INTRODUCTION

Begin the session by telling children that the story they are going to hear is about a mouse named Tom Thumb and his wife, Hunca Munca.

FIRST READING AND SHARING OF RESPONSES

Ask children to listen as you read the story aloud. When you first come to the words "perambulator," "nursery," "it was not fast," "frugal," and "bolster," explain them briefly, using the definitions given in the margin of your text.

After the reading, allow a few moments to clear up unfamiliar vocabulary and to let students ask questions and share their initial reactions to the story. Encourage children to offer their opinions about which parts of the story they especially liked and why, in preparation for the art activity.

ART ACTIVITY

Have the class turn to the frontispiece, captioned "I liked Tom Thumb and Hunca Munca most when they . . . ." Tell children that they are going to draw a picture of the part of the story where they liked Tom Thumb and Hunca Munca the most. As children draw, circulate among them and help them complete their captions.

Allow time for students to share and compare their drawings.

SESSION 2

POSTING "MY QUESTIONS"

Have students cut out the questions they wrote at home and pin them on the Sharing Questions bulletin board. Children who have not had an at-home reading can dictate their questions to you at this time. Encourage children to look at the Sharing Questions bulletin board during the week, to point out their own questions and to ask about those of their classmates.

READING AND REVIEW OF G.B.'S QUESTIONS

Read the story aloud, encouraging children to follow along in their books if they can. Pause to collect students' responses to G.B.'s questions (pages 10, 16, and 20). Help students think further about their responses by asking follow-up questions such as those given in the margin of your text.

SESSION 2 (continued)

ART ACTIVITY

Have the class turn to the page captioned "Hunca Munca also brought back...." Ask students to recall some of the things Hunca Munca brought back from the doll's-house, such as the bolster, a cradle, clothing, two chairs, and some useful pots and pans. Remind children that she also brought back several *other* things that are not named in the story. Tell the class they are going to draw a picture of what other things they think Hunca Munca brought back with her from the doll's-house. Help students get ideas for their drawings by asking such questions as *What things might Lucinda and Jane have had that Hunca Munca did not? Did Hunca Munca bring back something useful, or something pretty to decorate the mouse-hole?*

As children draw, circulate among them and help them complete their captions. Allow time for students to share and compare their drawings.

SESSION 3

ART ACTIVITY

Introduce the activity by telling children that every person in the world gets angry sometimes. In "The Tale of Two Bad Mice," Hunca Munca and Tom Thumb felt so disappointed when they found out the food was fake that they tore up the doll's-house to make themselves feel better. Ask children to think about a time when they, like the mice, felt disappointed and angry. If children need help getting started, ask for a few examples.

Then have students turn to the facing pages captioned "What Made Me Angry" and "What I Did to Feel Better." Ask them to draw one picture showing what they were disappointed or angry about, and another showing what they did to make themselves feel better.

Have children share their drawings only if they wish. It is not necessary for them to do so in order for the activity to help them sympathize with the mice and their "bad" behavior.

DRAMATIZATION

Tell the class they will be acting out the end of the story, when Tom Thumb and Hunca Munca make up for being naughty. Remind children that Tom Thumb and Hunca Munca stuff a sixpence in one of the stockings of Lucinda and Jane, and Hunca Munca sweeps the doll's-house every morning while everyone else is still asleep.

SESSION 3 (continued)

For the first scene, children will act out the parts of the two mice as they sneak into the doll's-house on Christmas Eve. Help the class set the scene by asking such questions as *Are Tom Thumb and Hunca Munca happy or nervous about going back to the doll's-house? What do you think the house is like in the middle of the night on Christmas Eve? How do the mice move across the nursery floor on their way to the doll's-house? What kinds of things do they see?* In a similar fashion, help children imagine the second scene, in which Hunca Munca sweeps the doll's-house.

Then divide the class into pairs for the first scene—assigning each student the role of either Tom Thumb or Hunca Munca—and have the groups improvise the scene together as a class. For the second scene, all the children can play the role of Hunca Munca, improvising the scene together as a class.

SESSION 4

SHARING QUESTIONS DISCUSSION

Prepare for discussion as usual, deciding on the five or six interpretive questions you intend to ask the class. Note which of the children's questions are similar to those you plan to lead and try to include three or four of their questions in your final list. When you write your questions on the board, include children's names as appropriate.

Suggested Interpretive Questions

Why does the pretend food make Tom Thumb and Hunca Munca so angry that they tear up the doll's-house?

Why do the mice think it's all right to take things from the doll's-house?

Why does the little girl think that a policeman doll is a good way to protect the doll's-house?

Why do Tom Thumb and Hunca Munca make up for being bad by giving the dolls money and sweeping the doll's-house every day?

ART ACTIVITY

Have the class turn to the page captioned "How do Hunca Munca and Tom Thumb feel about the policeman?" and tell children that they will be drawing an answer to this question. Help children think about the effect the policeman has on the two mice by asking such questions as *Are the two mice afraid of the policeman? Do they think he is watching what they do, or do they think he is fake like the food? Do you think the mice make up for their naughtiness because the policeman is there?*

Allow time for children to share and compare their drawings.

THE TALE
OF TWO
BAD MICE

BEATRIX POTTER

Hunca Munca also brought back _____

_____

Once upon a time there was a very
beautiful doll's-house; it was red brick
with white windows, and it had real
muslin curtains and a front door
and a chimney.

It belonged to two Dolls called
Lucinda and Jane, at least it belonged to
Lucinda, but she never ordered meals.

Jane was the Cook; but she never did
any cooking, because the dinner had been
bought ready-made, in a box full of
shavings.

There were two red lobsters and a
ham, a fish, a pudding, and some pears
and oranges.

They would not come off the plates,
but they were extremely beautiful.

One morning Lucinda and Jane had gone out for a drive in the doll's perambulator. There was no one in the nursery, and it was very quiet. Presently there was a little scuffling, scratching noise in a corner near the fireplace, where there was a hole under the skirting board.

Tom Thumb put out his head for a moment, and then popped it in again.

Tom Thumb was a mouse.

perambulator: a baby carriage

nursery: a child's bedroom

A minute afterwards, Hunca Munca, his wife, put her head out, too; and when she saw that there was no one in the nursery, she ventured out on the oilcloth under the coalbox.

The doll's-house stood at the other side of the fireplace. Tom Thumb and Hunca Munca went cautiously across the hearthrug. They pushed the front door— it was not fast.

it was not fast: it was not locked

Why do Hunca Munca and Tom Thumb go into the doll's-house? (Circle your favorite answer.)

1. They are curious.

2. They think it's for them.

3. They are looking for mischief.

4. Other _____

_____

Why don't the mice worry about going into a house that belongs to someone else?

Do the two mice think they are doing anything wrong when they go into the house?

Do the mice just want to see what's inside the house, or are they looking for something to take?

10

Tom Thumb and Hunca Munca went
upstairs and peeped into the dining room.
Then they squeaked with joy!

Such a lovely dinner was laid out
upon the table! There were tin spoons,
and lead knives and forks, and two
dolly-chairs—all *so* convenient!

Tom Thumb set to work at once to
carve the ham. It was a beautiful shiny
yellow, streaked with red.

The knife crumpled up and hurt him; he put his finger in his mouth.

"It is not boiled enough; it is hard. You have a try, Hunca Munca."

Hunca Munca stood up in her chair, and chopped at the ham with another lead knife.

"It's as hard as the hams at the cheesemonger's," said Hunca Munca.

The ham broke off the plate with a jerk, and rolled under the table.

"Let it alone," said Tom Thumb;
"give me some fish, Hunca Munca!"

Hunca Munca tried every tin spoon
in turn; the fish was glued to the dish.

Then Tom Thumb lost his temper.
He put the ham in the middle of the floor,
and hit it with the tongs and with the
shovel—bang, bang, smash, smash!

The ham flew all into pieces, for
underneath the shiny paint it was made
of nothing but plaster!

Then there was no end to the rage
and disappointment of Tom Thumb
and Hunca Munca. They broke up the
pudding, the lobsters, the pears and
the oranges.

As the fish would not come off the
plate, they put it into the red-hot crinkly
paper fire in the kitchen; but it would
not burn either.

Tom Thumb went up the kitchen
chimney and looked out at the top—there
was no soot.

While Tom Thumb was up the chimney,
Hunca Munca had another disappointment.
She found some tiny canisters upon
the dresser, labelled—Rice—Coffee—Sago—
but when she turned them upside down,
there was nothing inside except red
and blue beads.

Then those mice set to work to do
all the mischief they could—especially
Tom Thumb! He took Jane's clothes out of
the chest of drawers in her bedroom,
and he threw them out of the top floor
window.

Why do the angry
mice decide to do
all the mischief
they can?

*Why does the fake food
make the mice so mad?*

*Why does Tom Thumb
throw the doll's clothes out
the window?*

*Do you think the mice are
having fun when they do
their mischief?*

But Hunca Munca had a frugal mind.
After pulling half the feathers out of
Lucinda's bolster, she remembered that
she herself was in want of a feather bed.

With Tom Thumb's assistance she
carried the bolster downstairs, and across
the hearthrug. It was difficult to squeeze
the bolster into the mouse-hole; but they
managed it somehow.

frugal: knowing
how to save and use
things wisely

bolster: a long
pillow or cushion

17

Then Hunca Munca went back and
fetched a chair, a bookcase, a birdcage,
and several small odds and ends.
The bookcase and the birdcage refused
to go into the mouse-hole.

Hunca Munca left them behind the
coalbox, and went to fetch a cradle.

Hunca Munca was just returning with another chair, when suddenly there was a noise of talking outside upon the landing. The mice rushed back to their hole, and the dolls came into the nursery.

What a sight met the eyes of Jane and Lucinda! Lucinda sat upon the upset kitchen stove and stared; and Jane leant against the kitchen dresser and smiled— but neither of them made any remark.

The bookcase and the birdcage
were rescued from under the coalbox—
but Hunca Munca has got the cradle,
and some of Lucinda's clothes.

　　She also has some useful pots and
pans, and several other things.

Why does Hunca Munca think it's all right to keep the dolls' things?

Does Hunca Munca think that she needs these things more than the dolls do?

Why does she mostly take useful things, rather than pretty doll's-house things?

Does Hunca Munca take these things to make up for her disappointment in the fake food?

Hunca Munca also brought back _____

_____

The little girl that the doll's-house belonged to said, "I will get a doll dressed like a policeman!"

But the nurse said, "I will set a mousetrap!"

So that is the story of the two Bad Mice—but they were not so very very naughty after all, because Tom Thumb paid for everything he broke.

He found a crooked sixpence under the hearthrug; and upon Christmas Eve, he and Hunca Munca stuffed it into one of the stockings of Lucinda and Jane.

And very early every morning— before anybody is awake—Hunca Munca comes with her dustpan and her broom to sweep the Dollies' house!

What Made Me Angry

What I Did to Feel Better

How do Hunca Munca and Tom Thumb feel about the policeman?

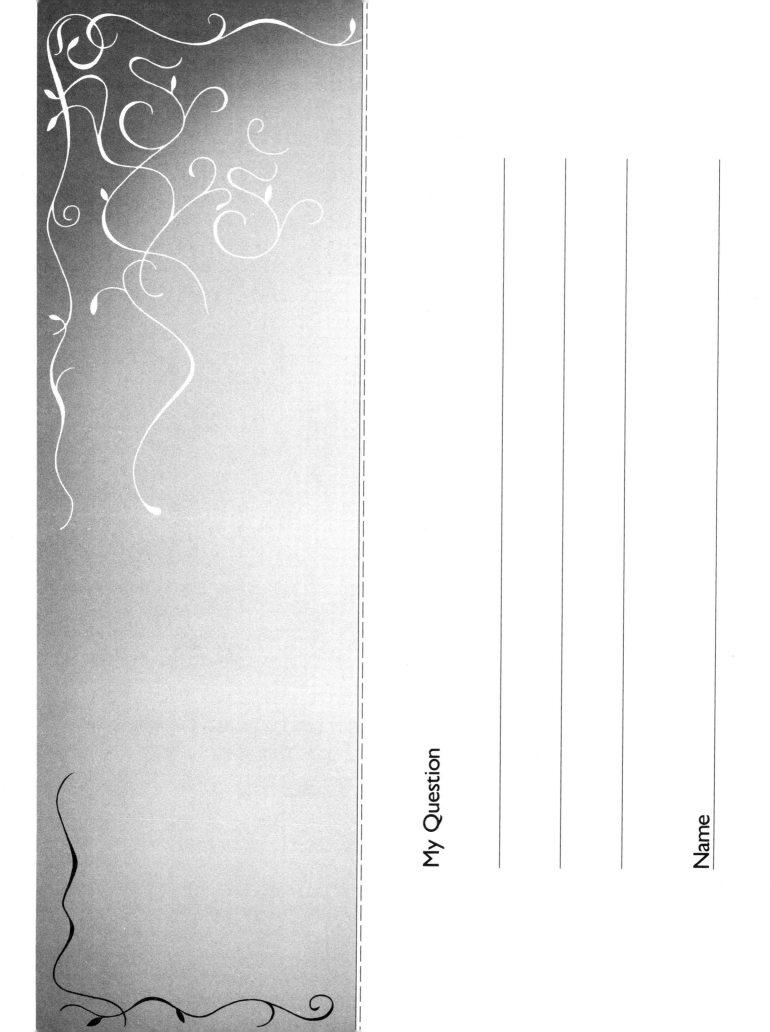

My Question

Name

BOUKI CUTS WOOD

HAITIAN FOLKTALE

AS TOLD BY

HAROLD COURLANDER

SESSION 1

INTRODUCTION

Begin the session by telling children that this is a Haitian story about a man named Bouki, who mistakes a traveler for a *bocor,* or *diviner*—a person who can tell what will happen in the future. Also show the class the illustration of Bouki in the tree and ask students what will happen to Bouki if he chops through the branch.

FIRST READING AND SHARING OF RESPONSES

Ask children to listen as you read the story aloud. When you first come to the words "machete," "foretell," "predicted," "bray," and "avocado," explain them briefly, using the definitions given in the margin of your text.

After the reading, allow a few moments to clear up unfamiliar vocabulary and to let students ask questions and share their initial reactions to the story. Encourage children to offer their opinions about which parts of the story they especially liked and why, in preparation for the art activity.

ART ACTIVITY

Have children turn to the frontispiece, captioned "I think it's funniest when...." Tell them that they are going to draw a picture of the part of the story that they think is the funniest.

As children draw, circulate among them and help them complete their captions. Allow time for students to share and compare their drawings.

SESSION 2

POSTING "MY QUESTIONS"

Have students cut out the questions they wrote at home and pin them on the Sharing Questions bulletin board. Children who have not had an at-home reading can dictate their questions to you at this time. Encourage children to look at the Sharing Questions bulletin board during the week, to point out their own questions and to ask about those of their classmates.

READING AND REVIEW OF G.B.'S QUESTIONS

Read the story aloud, encouraging children to follow along in their books if they can. Pause to collect students' responses to G.B.'s questions (pages 32, 35, and 38). Help students think further about their responses by asking follow-up questions such as those given in the margin of your text.

SESSION 2 (continued)

ART ACTIVITY

Have the class turn to the page captioned "Bouki! You're not dead!" Ask children to imagine what *they* would do to convince Bouki that he's not dead and that he should get up and start acting alive. Help students get ideas for their drawings by asking them such questions as *What might you do to Bouki that would convince him to start acting alive? Could you convince him by yourself, or would you need other people? What is something that's so much fun to do that you don't think anyone could resist doing it?*

Allow time for children to share and compare their drawings.

SESSION 3

DRAMATIZATION

Tell the class that they will be acting out the story, from when the donkey starts braying to the end.

Choose one child to play Bouki and another to play the donkey. Divide the rest of the class into two groups of farmers. Help children prepare for their roles by asking such questions as *How do you think Bouki felt when he lay on the ground without moving? How did the farmers feel when they thought "old Bouki" was dead? Why do the farmers drop Bouki and run away when they hear him sneeze and talk? What does Bouki look like when he jumps up and takes the avocado from the donkey?*

Then read aloud from page 33 to the end of the story. As you read, allow students time to perform the actions of Bouki, the donkey, and the farmers.

SHARING QUESTIONS DISCUSSION

Prepare for discussion as usual, deciding on the five or six interpretive questions you intend to ask the class. Note which of the children's questions are similar to those you plan to lead and try to include three or four of their questions in your final list. When you write your questions on the board, include children's names as appropriate.

Suggested Interpretive Questions

Why does Bouki believe he is dead when he feels alive?

Why does Bouki want to know when he will die?

Why does Bouki stop acting dead long enough to point out the correct way to his house?

Why don't the farmers who find Bouki realize he isn't dead when they hear him sneeze and talk?

SESSION 4

DRAMATIZATION

Tell the class they will be thinking about what it was like for Bouki to lie motionless at the side of the trail. Remind children that Bouki lay very still and went a long time without talking, but he could still hear, feel, and think things.

Then have children lie on the floor or put their heads down on their desks, and ask them to close their eyes. As students lie motionless, encourage them to notice the different kinds of sensations they have, such as feeling the floor beneath them, feeling their own breathing and heartbeat, hearing sounds outside and inside the classroom, or "seeing" colors behind their closed eyes.

After a minute or two, have the class gather in a group to share briefly their different sensations. Conclude the discussion by asking children *What kinds of things do you think should have told Bouki that he was really alive?*

GROUP CREATIVE WRITING

Tell children they are going to write a poem about the different things that tell them they are alive, even when they are lying very still. Write on the board or chart paper the title "When I Am Very Still" and the first line, "When I am lying very still with my eyes shut." Read the line aloud and tell students that together they are going to add some more lines to the poem, describing the different things they could hear and feel when they lay motionless.

Have children offer examples of the different sensations they experienced when they were lying still, such as what they heard, smelled, and felt. Write their responses on the board or chart paper, following the pattern given in the student book. You might combine several examples of the same sensation in one line.

When the poem is completed, read it back to the class. Make copies for students to paste into their books on the page provided, or help them copy their favorite lines.

Here is an example of a poem that a class might compose:

When I Am Very Still

When I am lying very still with my eyes shut,
I can hear kids playing outside, cars honking,
     and doors squeaking.
I can feel my heart beating, my nose itching.
I can smell lunch cooking in the cafeteria.
I can taste it already.
When I am very still.

BOUKI CUTS WOOD

HAITIAN FOLKTALE

I think it's funniest when _____

Bouki went out to cut wood in the Pine Forest. He climbed a tree, sat on a branch, and began to chop with his machete. A traveler came along and stopped to watch him. "Wye!" the man said. "Just look at that! He's sitting on the same branch that he's cutting. In a few minutes the branch will fall, and he'll be on the ground. How foolish can a person be?"

machete: a long knife with a wide blade, like a sword

Bouki stopped chopping. "Who is the stupid man that calls me foolish?" he called down. "Are you trying to foretell the future? Only God knows what is going to happen."

foretell: tell what is going to happen in the future

31

The traveler said no more. He went on his way.

Bouki resumed his chopping. Just as the man predicted, the branch broke, and Bouki came down with it.

Bouki gave it some thought. "It was just as the man predicted," Bouki said. "He must be a *bocor,* a diviner."

He jumped on his donkey and rode after the man. When he caught up with him on the trail, he said, *"Bocor,* you told the truth. I didn't know you were a diviner. You predicted the future, and it came out just as you said. So tell me one more thing: When am I going to die?"

The traveler answered, "Who in his right mind wants to know that? But if you insist, I'll tell you." He thought for a moment. "You'll die when your donkey brays three times," he said, and continued on his way.

predicted: said would happen

bray: the sound a donkey makes

Why does the traveler tell Bouki he will die when his donkey brays three times?

Why doesn't the traveler explain to Bouki that he is not a bocor? Why doesn't he explain how he was able to "predict" Bouki's fall?

32

What does the traveler mean when he says that no one in his right mind would want to know when he is going to die?

"Thank you, *bocor,* thank you!"
Bouki called after him. Then he said to
himself, "Three times! This donkey
is braying all the time!"

And as soon as they started back, the
donkey opened his mouth and brayed.

"Stop! That's one already!" Bouki
shouted.

The donkey brayed again.

"Stop! Stop! That's twice already!"
Bouki shouted.

And as the donkey opened its
mouth and stretched its neck to bray again,
Bouki leaned over the animal's head
and tried to push its jaws together.
He struggled. The donkey struggled.
Then it came—another bray.

"That's the end," Bouki said.
"He brayed three times! Therefore,
I must be dead!"

So he fell off the donkey and lay
motionless at the side of the trail.
He didn't try to get up because dead
men lie where they fall.

After a while some farmers came
along. "There is Bouki sleeping on
the trail," one of them said.

"No," another one said, poking Bouki with his hoe, "he must be dead."

They sat him up, but he fell down again.

"Yes," they said, "old Bouki is finished. We'll have to take him home."

They picked him up and carried him, feet first, head behind. As they walked, the donkey followed and sniffed at Bouki's face. Bouki sneezed. When the men heard that, they dropped Bouki on the ground and ran.

Why does Bouki still think he's dead even after he sneezes? (Circle your favorite answer.)

1. He's stubborn.

2. He doesn't trust his own eyes and ears.

3. He's silly.

4. Other _____

_____

_____

What are some things that should let Bouki know he is alive? Why does he ignore these things?

Why doesn't Bouki just decide that the traveler must have been wrong?

35

Bouki lay without moving. Some other farmers came along. "Look!" they said, "Old Bouki is dead!"

They also picked him up and carried him. After a little while they stopped. "Which trail goes to Bouki's house?" one of them asked.

"That one between the trees," another one said.

And another answered, "No, it's straight ahead."

They put Bouki on the ground
while they argued. "This way," one said.
"That way," another said.

Finally, without opening his eyes,
Bouki moved his arm slowly until
it pointed back the way they had come.

"It's not proper for the dead to argue,"
he said. "But all of you are wrong.
We passed my trail way back there."

The farmers took a quick look at
Bouki and began to run. Again he
was alone. No one came. He lay patiently.
After a while he felt a sensation in his
stomach. "If I was alive," he thought,
"that would mean that I'm hungry.
But as I'm dead, I must be mistaken."

After a while he opened one eye
slowly. He saw his donkey nuzzling
an avocado that had fallen from a tree.

avocado: a
green fruit

37

"Leave it!" Bouki shouted.
He jumped to his feet and snatched
the avocado away from the donkey.
He opened it and ate.

Then he got on his donkey and
started home. "**Dead or not**," he said,
"**I need a big bowl of rice and beans.**"

Why does it take
hunger to make
Bouki stop acting
like a dead man?

*Why does Bouki at
first think he's
mistaken when he
feels hungry?*

*Why does Bouki
decide that he
really **is** hungry
when he sees the
donkey about to
eat the avocado?*

*Why does eating
the avocado make
Bouki think he
might be alive,
when being poked
with the hoe and
sneezing did not?*

*Why is Bouki still
confused about
whether or not he
is alive?*

Bouki! You're not dead!

When I Am Very Still

When I am lying very still with my eyes shut,

I can hear _____

I can feel _____

I can smell _____

I can _____

When I am very still.

My Question

_____

_____

_____

Name _____

FANTASY

POETRY BY
SYLVIA PLATH,
EDWARD LEAR,
AND
LEWIS CARROLL

SESSION 1: "The Bed Book"

This session consists of an introduction, two readings of the poem, and an art activity in which children draw a picture of a fantasy bed.

AT-HOME WORK: "The Bed Book"

The adult partner reads the poem through once, encouraging the child to join in saying the underlined words and phrases. The adult then reads the poem a second time, pausing to discuss G.B.'s three questions. When called for, children respond to these questions by circling their answer or by circling parts of the poem.

After reading, the adult writes the child's own question about "The Bed Book" into the book.

SESSION 2: "The Bed Book"

During this reading of the poem, you will collect students' responses to G.B.'s questions and lead a discussion of them. The session concludes with a group creative writing activity in which children compose a poem about the right sort of imaginary beds for different kinds of people.

SESSION 3: "The Table and the Chair"

This session consists of an introduction and first reading of the poem, a second reading with textual analysis, and a dramatization.

SESSION 4: "The Lobster Quadrille"

This session consists of an introduction and first reading of the poem, a second reading with textual analysis, a dramatization in which children dance the Lobster Quadrille, and an art activity in which students draw their interpretation of their favorite dancing sea creature.

SESSION 1: "The Bed Book"

INTRODUCTION

Introduce the poem by telling children that it is about fantasy beds.

FIRST AND SECOND READINGS

Ask children to listen as you read the poem aloud. Before reading the poem a second time, take a few moments to let children ask questions and make comments. Also help children clear up such unfamiliar vocabulary as "Troupe of Acrobats," "automat," "shillings," "Hottentot," and "hollyhock," using the definitions given in the margin of your text.

Read the poem aloud a second time, encouraging students to follow along in their books if they can, and to join in saying the underlined words and phrases.

ART ACTIVITY

Have students turn to the frontispiece, captioned "The most special bed is...." Tell them that they are going to draw a picture showing the kind of bed they would most like to have. Have the class briefly recall some of the beds described in the poem. Let children know that they can draw a favorite bed from the poem or a fantasy bed of their own.

As children draw, circulate among them and help them complete their captions. Allow time for students to share and compare their drawings.

SESSION 2: "The Bed Book"

POSTING "MY QUESTIONS"

Have students cut out the questions they wrote at home. Glance through them briefly and note any that you might want to raise during your discussion of G.B.'s questions. Then pin students' questions on the Sharing Questions bulletin board. Let children know that even though there will be no Sharing Questions Discussion this week, they should still look at the bulletin board and talk about their questions with each other.

READING AND REVIEW OF G.B.'S QUESTIONS

Read the poem aloud, pausing to collect students' responses to G.B.'s questions. Ask children to give reasons for their answers, and then help them think further about the poem by asking additional questions such as those given in the margin of your text.

GROUP CREATIVE WRITING

Tell children that they will be writing a poem about the right sort of beds for different kinds of people. Write on the board or a piece of chart paper the poem's title and outline, as follows:

The Right Sort of Bed

A person who is always cheerful,

Has a bed_____

SESSION 2: "The Bed Book" (continued)

Help students get started by asking them to think about the kind of imaginary bed that a cheerful person might have. As children offer their suggestions, write them on the board to form the second line of the stanza.

Continue adding two-line stanzas following the pattern given in the student book. If students need help thinking of different kinds of people for the first lines, provide a few examples of your own, such as "A person who likes sports" or "A person who likes sweets."

When the poem is finished, read it back to the class. Make copies for students to paste into their books on the page titled "The Right Sort of Bed," or help them copy their favorite stanza on the lines provided.

If time allows, children may use the remaining space on the page to illustrate their favorite stanza.

Here is an example of a poem that a class might compose:

The Right Sort of Bed

A person who is always cheerful,
Has a bed that looks like a great big smile,
   and has a pillow that giggles;

A person who likes sports,
Has a bed in the shape of a baseball mitt;

A person who likes sweets,
Has a bed with lollipop legs, a cake mattress,
   and jelly doughnut pillows;

A person who likes to do things slowly,
Has a bed on the back of a turtle;

And a person who likes to do things quickly,
Has a bed with eagle's wings or roller skates.

SESSION 3: "The Table and the Chair"

INTRODUCTION

Introduce the poem by telling students that it is about a special table and chair that decide to take a walk to town.

FIRST READING

Have children listen while you read the poem through once. Then take a few moments to let children ask questions and make comments. Also help children clear up such unfamiliar vocabulary as "chilblains" and "toddle," using the definitions given in the margin of your text.

SECOND READING AND TEXTUAL ANALYSIS

Read the poem aloud a second time, encouraging students to follow along in their books if they can, and to join in saying the last four lines. During this second reading, pause to conduct a textual analysis, using questions such as those printed in your text.

SESSION 3: "The Table and the Chair" (continued)

DRAMATIZATION

Tell children they are going to act out the poem. Help students prepare by having them practice the way they think the table and chair would walk around on two legs. Then have students act out the poem as you read it through. If they like, some students can play the Ducky, the Mouse, and the Beetle.

If time permits, children might enjoy thinking about how other kinds of furniture, such as a couch or a lamp, might move, and performing a "furniture parade."

SESSION 4: "The Lobster Quadrille"

INTRODUCTION

Introduce the poem by telling children that it is about a snail that is invited to join other sea creatures in a very lively square dance called a *quadrille*. Explain that a *lobster* is a shellfish with big claws, and a *whiting* is a common fish that people eat. You may want to take a moment to show children the illustrations and identify the various sea creatures named in the poem.

FIRST READING

Have children listen while you read the poem through once. Then take a few moments to let children ask questions and make comments. Also help children clear up such unfamiliar vocabulary as "porpoise," "shingle," and "askance," using the definitions given in the margin of your text.

SECOND READING AND TEXTUAL ANALYSIS

Read the poem aloud a second time, encouraging students to follow along in their books if they can, and to join in saying the underlined phrases. During the second reading, pause at the end of each stanza to conduct a textual analysis, using questions such as those printed in your text.

DRAMATIZATION

Tell children that they are going to dance the Lobster Quadrille. Have the class form two straight lines, facing each other. Then read the poem aloud as children clap out the rhythm. When you come to the refrain at the end of each stanza, have children repeat it with you. During the first line of the refrain, children will move toward each other, meet in the middle, and bow. During the second line of the refrain, they will move back to their original positions.

ART ACTIVITY

Have children turn to the page captioned "My favorite dancing sea creature is the…." Tell them that they are going to draw a picture of the sea creature they would most like to see dancing on the rocky shore. Let students know that they can add imaginative details, such as clothes or facial expressions, to show what kind of personality they think that creature has.

As children draw, circulate among them and help them complete their captions. Allow time for children to share and compare their drawings.

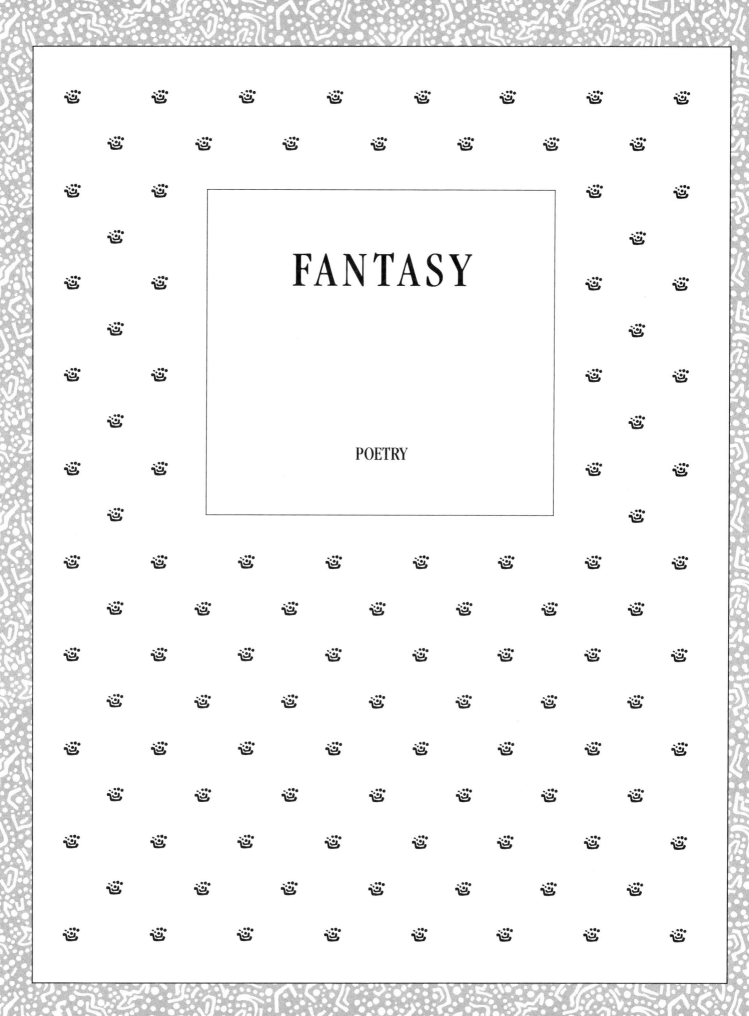

FANTASY

POETRY

The most special bed is _____

THE BED BOOK

BEDS come in all sizes—
Single or double,
Cot-size or cradle,
King-size or trundle.

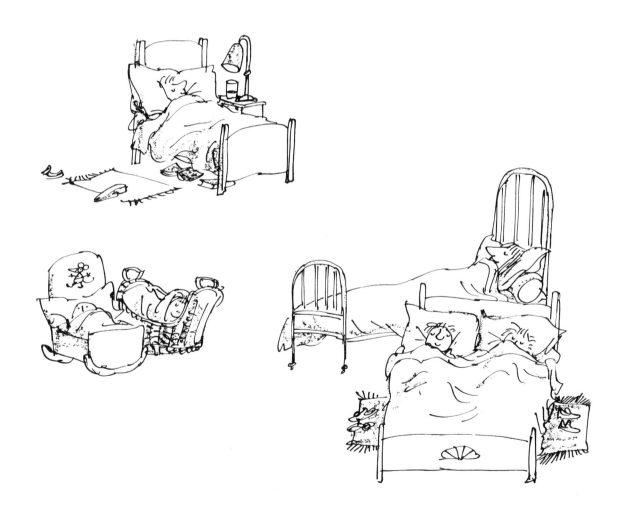

Most Beds are Beds
For sleeping or resting,
But the *best* Beds are much
More interesting!

Not just a white little
Tucked-in-tight little
Nighty-night little
Turn-out-the-light little
Bed—

Instead
A Bed for Fishing,
A Bed for Cats,
A Bed for a Troupe of
Acrobats.

Troupe of Acrobats: a group of performers who do things like tumbles and flips

47

The *right* sort of Bed
(If you see what I mean)
Is a Bed that might
Be a Submarine

Nosing through water
Clear and green,
Silver and glittery
As a sardine

Or a Jet-Propelled Bed
For visiting Mars
With mosquito nets
For the shooting stars.

Would you
rather have a
Submarine Bed or a
Jet-Propelled Bed?
(Circle your answer.)

A SUBMARINE BED

A JET-PROPELLED
   BED

Why?

*Where would this bed be
able to take you? What
things would you see?*

*How would it feel to ride
in this bed?*

*What would be most fun
about this bed?*

If you get hungry
In the middle of the night
A Snack Bed is good
For the appetite—

With a pillow of bread
To nibble at
And up at the head
An automat

automat: a place where you can buy food from machines

shillings: British money

Where you need no shillings,
Just a finger to stick in
The slot, and out come
Cakes and cold chicken.

Another Bed
That fills the bill
Is the sort of Bed
That is Spottable—

With blankets all splotches
Of black, blue and pink
So nobody'll notice
If you spill ink

Or if the dog and the cat
And the parakeet
Dance on the covers
With muddyish feet.

In a Spottable Bed
It *never* matters
Where jam rambles
And where paint splatters!

On the other hand,
If you want to *move*
A Tank Bed's the Bed
Most movers approve.

A Tank Bed's got cranks
And wheels and cogs
And levers to pull
If you're stuck in bogs.

A Tank Bed's treads
Go upstairs or down
Through duck ponds or through
A cobbledy town.

And you're snug inside
If it rains or hails.
A Tank Bed's got
Everything but sails!

Now a gentler Bed
Is a good deal more
The sort of Bed
Bird-Watchers adore—

A kind of hammock
Between two tall trees
Where you can swing
In the leaves at ease

And count all the birds—
Wren, robin and rook—
And write their names
In a Naming Book.

Around Bird-Watching Beds
You hang nests of straw
For hummingbirds, hoopoes
And the great macaw.

All the birds would flock
(If I'm not mistaken)
To your berries and cherries
And bits of bacon.

None of these Beds,
Of course, is very
Easy to fold up
Or fetch and carry

So a Pocket-size Bed
Is a fine Bed to own.
When you're eating out
With friend Jim or Aunt Joan

And they say: ***It's too bad***

You can't stay overnight

But there isn't an extra

Bed in sight.

You can take out your Bed
Shrunk small as a pea
And water it till
It grows suitably.

Yes, a Pocket-size Bed
Works very well
Only how can you tell,
O how can you tell

It won't shrink back
To the size of a pea
While you're asleep in it?
Then where would you be!

On these two pages, circle what you would like most about an Elephant Bed.

Where would you tell your Elephant Bed to take you?

In what other ways might your Elephant Bed make you feel safe?

What other games could you play on your Elephant Bed?

O here is a Bed
Shrinkproofer than that,
A floatier, boatier
Bed than that!

In an Elephant Bed
You go where you please.
You pick bananas
Right out of the trees.

If the tigers jump up
When you happen to sneeze
Why, they can't jump higher
Than the elephant's knees.

An Elephant Bed
Is where kings ride.
It's cool as a pool
In the shade inside.

You can climb up the trunk
And slide down behind.
Everyone knows
Elephants don't mind!—

When it's even too hot
For the Hottentot
A trunk-spray shower's
There on the spot.

Hottentot: a people who live in southern Africa, where it is very hot

But when it's lots
Of degrees below,
A North-Pole Bed
Is the best I know.

It's warm as toast
Under ten feet of snow.
It's warm as the Bed
Of an Eskimo.

A North-Pole Bed
Is made of fur.
It's fine if you're
An ex-plor-er,

Or if you just
Have a very cold nose.
There's a built-in oven
To warm your toes.

O who cares much
If a Bed's big or small
Or lumpy and bumpy—
Who cares at all

60

As long as its springs
Are bouncy and new.
From a Bounceable Bed
You bounce into the blue—

Over the hollyhocks

hollyhock: a tall plant with beautiful flowers

(**Toodle-oo!**)
Over the owls'
To-whit-to-whoo,

Over the moon
To Timbuktoo
With springier springs
Than a kangaroo.

You can see if the Big Dipper's
Full of stew,
And you may want to stay
Up a week or two.

These are the **Beds**
For me and for you!
These are the **Beds**
To climb into:

Pocket-size **Beds**
And **Beds** for Snacks,
Tank **Beds**, **Beds**
On Elephant Backs,

Beds that fly,
Or go under water,
Bouncy **Beds**, **Beds**
You can Spatter and Spotter,

Bird-Watching **Beds**,
Beds for zero weather—
Any kind of **Bed**
As long as it's rather

Special and queer
And full of surprises—
Beds of amazing
Shapes and sizes,

NOT just a white little
Tucked-in-tight little
Nighty-night little
Turn-out-the-light little
Bed!

—Sylvia Plath

What's wrong with a bed that is just for sleeping or resting?

Why do you think a bed should be for more than just sleeping?

How would you change your bed at home to make it more fun?

Do you think you would ever get any sleep if you had a really fun bed?

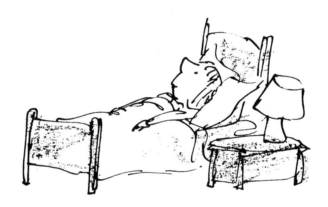

The Right Sort of Bed

A person who _____

Has a bed _____

My Question

_____

_____

_____

Name _____

THE TABLE AND THE CHAIR

1

Said the Table to the Chair,
"You can hardly be aware,
How I suffer from the heat,
And from chilblains on my feet!
If we took a little walk,
We might have a little talk!
Pray let us take the air!"
Said the Table to the Chair.

chilblains: swellings or sores caused by the cold

Textual Analysis Question

Why does the Table think it can take a little walk with the Chair?

2

Said the Chair unto the Table,

"Now you *know* we are not able!

How foolishly you talk,

When you know we *cannot* walk!"

Said the Table, with a sigh,

"It can do no harm to try,

I've as many legs as you,

Why can't we walk on two?"

Textual Analysis Questions

Why does the Chair think that they *cannot* walk?

3

So they both went slowly down,

And walked about the town

With a cheerful bumpy sound,

As they toddled round and round.

And everybody cried,

As they hastened to their side,

"See! the Table and the Chair

Have come out to take the air!"

toddle: to walk with short, unsteady steps

What would you think if you saw a table and a chair walking down the street?

71

4

But in going down an alley,

To a castle in a valley,

They completely lost their way,

And wandered all the day,

Till, to see them safely back,

They paid a Ducky-quack,

And a Beetle, and a Mouse,

Who took them to their house.

5

Then they whispered to each other,
"O delightful little brother!
What a lovely walk we've taken!
Let us dine on Beans and Bacon!"
So the Ducky, and the leetle
Browny-Mousy and the Beetle
Dined, and danced upon their heads
Till they toddled to their beds.

—Edward Lear

Textual Analysis Question

Why do the Table and the Chair think they have had a lovely walk even though they got completely lost?

THE LOBSTER QUADRILLE

"Will you walk a little faster?"
    said a whiting to a snail.

porpoise: a small whale

"There's a porpoise close behind us,
    and he's treading on my tail.
See how eagerly the lobsters
    and the turtles all advance!

shingle: a stony beach

They are waiting on the shingle—
    will you come and join the dance?
**Will you, won't you, will you, won't you,
    will you join the dance?
Will you, won't you, will you, won't you,
    won't you join the dance?**

Textual Analysis Question

Why does the whiting invite the snail to come and join the dance?

74

"You can really have no notion
　　how delightful it will be,
When they take us up and throw us,
　　with the lobsters, out to sea!"
But the snail replied, "Too far, too far!"
　　and gave a look askance—
Said he thanked the whiting kindly,
　　but he would not join the dance.

Would not, could not, would not, could not,
　　would not join the dance.

Would not, could not, would not, could not,
　　could not join the dance.

Textual Analysis Questions

Why won't the snail join the dance? Why is he worried about being thrown too far out to sea?

"What matters it how far we go?"
    his scaly friend replied.
"There is another shore, you know,
    upon the other side.
The further off from England
    the nearer is to France—
Then turn not pale, beloved snail,
    but come and join the dance.
Will you, won't you, will you, won't you,
    will you join the dance?
Will you, won't you, will you, won't you,
    won't you join the dance?"

        —Lewis Carroll

Textual Analysis Question

Do you think the snail
should accept the whiting's
invitation to join the dance?

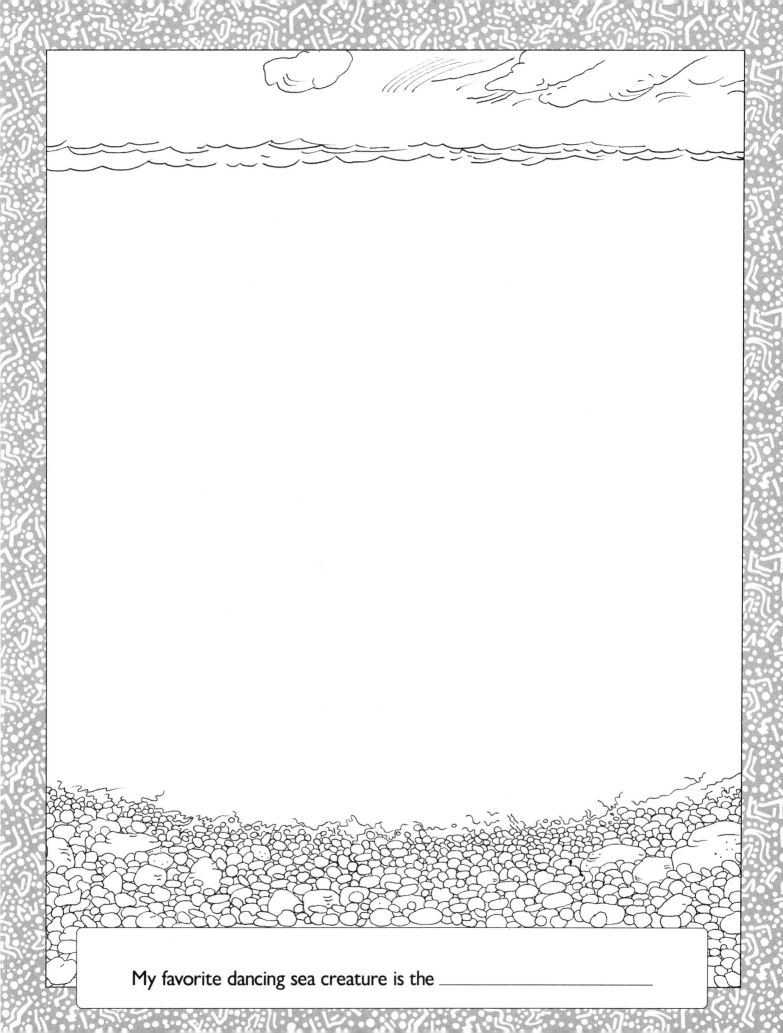

My favorite dancing sea creature is the _____

LION
AT
SCHOOL

PHILIPPA PEARCE

SESSION 1

This session consists of an introduction and first reading of the story, followed by a brief sharing of questions and comments, and an art activity in which children draw their interpretation of Noil, the lion, at school.

AT-HOME WORK

During this second reading, the adult partner pauses to discuss G.B.'s three questions. Children respond to the first question by circling their answer.

After reading, the adult writes the child's own question about the story into the book in preparation for the Sharing Questions Discussion (Session 4).

SESSION 2

During this reading of the story, you will collect students' responses to G.B.'s questions and lead a discussion of them. The session concludes with an art activity in which children create a mask showing their interpretation of the lion. See the Session 2 activities page for the necessary art materials.

SESSION 3

This session consists of a dramatization in which children play the lion when he frightens Jack Tall away, and an art activity in which students draw their interpretation of the little girl at the end of the story when she is back on the playground.

SESSION 4

This session consists of a Sharing Questions Discussion and an art activity in which students draw a picture showing where they would like to take the lion if he could be their friend for a day.

SESSION 1

INTRODUCTION

Begin the session by telling children that they are going to hear a story about a little girl named Betty Small, who meets a lion while walking to school one day.

FIRST READING AND SHARING OF RESPONSES

Ask children to listen as you read the story aloud. When you first come to the words "skewer," "register," "fish fingers," and "pale," explain them briefly, using the definitions given in the margin of your text.

After the reading, allow a few moments to clear up unfamiliar vocabulary and to let students ask questions and share their initial reactions to the story. Encourage children to offer their opinions about which parts of the story they especially liked and why, in preparation for the art activity.

ART ACTIVITY

Have children turn to the frontispiece, captioned "Lion at School." Tell them that they are going to draw a picture of the lion when he is at school with the little girl. Remind children that the lion is both fierce and friendly, and that their pictures might show him behaving either way. If children want, they can include in their drawings other characters in the story, such as the little girl, the teacher, other students, or Jack Tall.

Allow time for students to share and compare their drawings.

SESSION 2

POSTING "MY QUESTIONS"

Have students cut out the questions they wrote at home and pin them on the Sharing Questions bulletin board. Children who have not had an at-home reading can dictate their questions to you at this time. Encourage children to look at the Sharing Questions bulletin board during the week, to point out their own questions and to ask about those of their classmates.

READING AND REVIEW OF G.B.'S QUESTIONS

Read the story aloud, encouraging children to follow along in their books if they can. Pause to collect students' responses to G.B.'s questions (pages 9, 12, and 19). Help students think further about their responses by asking follow-up questions such as those given in the margin of your text.

SESSION 2 (continued)

ART ACTIVITY

Supply each student with drawing materials and a paper plate or piece of heavy paper. Have students make lion masks by cutting away a pie-shaped piece at the bottom of the plate to expose the mouth, and by cutting out holes for the eyes. You may want to prepare the plates in advance by marking them with a dotted line where students should cut, as in the drawing at left. Students can complete their masks by drawing a lion's snout and whiskers, snipping the edges of the plate to create a mane, or pasting on pieces of construction paper for ears and a mane.

SESSION 3

DRAMATIZATION

Tell students they will be acting out the part of the story where the lion roars at Jack Tall on the playground. Remind them that when the lion roared, the children in the story could see his teeth as sharp as skewers and knives and his throat as deep and dark as a tunnel, and that they had to plug their ears.

Help children prepare to play the lion by asking such questions as *How does the lion feel when he scares Jack Tall away? Why is Jack Tall so afraid of the lion that he runs away? Do you think Betty Small is afraid of the lion when he roars? How do you think Betty Small feels when the lion frightens Jack Tall away?*

Have children put on their lion masks. Then read aloud the passage on page 16 beginning, "After dinner all the children went into the playground," and ending on page 17, "He never stopped running until he got home to his mother." Encourage children to repeat the lion's lines and to act out growling, showing their teeth, and roaring.

ART ACTIVITY

Have the class turn to the page captioned "Back on the Playground." Tell children they are going to draw a picture of the little girl at the very end of the story when she is back on the playground. Help children get ideas for their drawings by asking such questions as *Do you think the little girl likes going to school now? Does she play with any of the other children on the playground? How do you think she feels when she talks to Jack Tall? Why does Jack Tall ask about the lion?*

Allow time for students to share and compare their drawings.

SESSION 4

SHARING QUESTIONS DISCUSSION

Prepare for discussion as usual, deciding on the five or six interpretive questions you intend to ask the class. Note which of the children's questions are similar to those you plan to lead and try to include three or four of their questions in your final list. When you write your questions on the board, include children's names as appropriate.

Suggested Interpretive Questions

Why does the lion want to go to school with the little girl?

Why does the lion insist that he is not a pet? Why does he prefer to be called the little girl's friend?

Why does the little girl want to ride to school on the lion's back?

Why does the little girl's fear of Jack Tall keep her from making friends with her classmates?

Why doesn't the lion stay for afternoon school, or come back to school on Monday?

ART ACTIVITY

Have the class turn to the page captioned "I would like to take the lion...." Tell children that they are going to draw a picture showing where they would take the lion if he could be their friend for a day. Explain that their drawings should include themselves together with the lion. If children need help getting started, have them briefly share a few ideas.

As children draw, circulate among them and help them complete their captions. Allow time for children to share and compare their drawings.

LION
AT
SCHOOL

PHILIPPA PEARCE

Lion at School

Once upon a time there was a little girl who didn't like going to school. She always set off late. Then she had to hurry, but she never hurried fast enough.

One morning she was hurrying along as usual when she turned a corner and there stood a lion, blocking her way. He stood waiting for her. He stared at her with his yellow eyes. He growled, and when he growled, the little girl could see that his teeth were as sharp as skewers and knives. He growled: "I'm going to eat you up."

skewer: a long, sharp piece of metal used to hold food while it's cooking

"Oh, dear!" said the little girl, and she began to cry.

"Wait!" said the lion. "I haven't finished. I'm going to eat you up UNLESS you take me to school with you."

"Oh, dear!" said the little girl. "I couldn't do that. My teacher says we mustn't bring pets to school."

"I'm not a pet," said the lion. He growled again, and she saw that his tail swished from side to side in anger— *swish! swash!* "You can tell your teacher that I'm a friend who is coming to school with you," he said. "Now shall we go?"

The little girl had stopped crying.
She said, "All right. But you must promise
two things. First of all, you mustn't eat
anyone; it's not allowed."

"I suppose I can growl?" said the lion.

"I suppose you can," said the little girl.

"And I suppose I can roar?"

"Must you?" said the little girl.

"Yes," said the lion.

"Then I suppose you can,"
said the little girl.

Why does the lion say that he is going to eat the little girl up unless she takes him to school?

What do you think is scary about the lion? Why does he want to make sure that he can growl and roar at school?

What would be fun about having a friend that can growl and roar like the lion?

Why does the little girl agree to let the lion growl and roar? (Circle your favorite answer.)

1. She's afraid to say "no" to the lion.

2. She knows that lions need to growl and roar.

3. She secretly wants her new friend to growl and roar.

4. Other _____ _____ _____

9

"And what's the second thing?"
asked the lion.

"You must let me ride on your back
to school."

"Very well," said the lion.

He crouched down on the pavement
and the little girl climbed onto his back.
She held on by his mane. Then they
went on together toward the school,
the little girl riding the lion.

The lion ran with the little girl on his
back to school. Even so, they were late.
The little girl and the lion went into the
classroom just as the teacher was
calling the register.

The teacher stopped calling the
register when she saw the little girl and
the lion. She stared at the lion, and all
the other children stared at the lion,

register: the roll,
listing all of the
students in the class

10

wondering what the teacher was going to say. The teacher said to the little girl, "You know you are not allowed to bring pets to school."

The lion began to swish his tail— *swish! swash!* The little girl said, "This is not a pet. This is my friend who is coming to school with me."

The teacher still stared at the lion, but she said to the little girl, "What is his name then?"

"Noil," said the little girl. "His name is Noil. Just Noil." She knew it would be no good to tell the teacher that her friend was a lion, so she had turned his name backward: LION—NOIL.

The teacher wrote the name down in the register: NOIL. Then she finished calling the register.

"Betty Small," she said.

"Yes," said the little girl.

"Noil," said the teacher.

"Yes," said the lion. He mumbled, opening his mouth as little as possible, so that the teacher should not see his teeth as sharp as skewers and knives.

All that morning the lion sat up on his chair next to the little girl, like a big cat, with his tail curled around his front paws, as good as gold. He didn't speak unless the teacher spoke to him. He didn't growl; he didn't roar.

Why is the lion "as good as gold" when he's at school?

Why doesn't the lion growl and roar in the classroom? Why does he hide his sharp teeth from the teacher?

Do you think the teacher or the other students are afraid of the lion?

How does the little girl feel about having the lion sit next to her?

12

At playtime the little girl and the lion
went into the playground. All the children
stopped playing to stare at the lion.
Then they went on playing again.
The little girl stood in a corner of the
playground, with the lion beside her.

"Why don't we play like the others?"
the lion asked.

The little girl said, "I don't like
playing because some of the big boys are
so big and rough. They knock you
over without meaning to."

The lion growled. "They wouldn't knock ME over," he said.

"There's one big boy—the very biggest," said the little girl. "His name is Jack Tall. He knocks me over on purpose."

"Which is he?" said the lion. "Point him out to me."

The little girl pointed out Jack Tall to the lion.

"Ah!" said the lion. "So that's Jack Tall."

Just then the bell rang again, and all the children went back to their classrooms. The lion went with the little girl and sat beside her.

Then the children drew and wrote until dinnertime. The lion was hungry, so he wanted to draw a picture of his dinner.

"What will it be for dinner?" he asked the little girl. "I hope it's meat."

"No," said the little girl. "It will be fish fingers because today is Friday."

Then the little girl showed the lion how to hold the yellow crayon in his paw and draw fish fingers. Underneath his picture she wrote: "I like meat better than fish fingers."

fish fingers:
breaded fish sticks

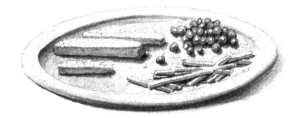

Then it was dinnertime. The lion sat up on his chair at the dinner table next to the little girl.

The lion ate very fast, and at the end he said, "I'm still hungry, and I wish it had been meat."

15

After dinner all the children went
into the playground.

All the big boys were running about,
and the very biggest boy, Jack Tall,
came running toward the little girl.
He was running in circles, closer and
closer to the little girl.

"Go away," said the lion. "You might
knock my friend over. Go away."

"Shan't," said Jack Tall. The little girl
got behind the lion.

Jack Tall was running closer and
closer and closer.

The lion growled. Then Jack Tall
saw the lion's teeth as sharp as skewers
and knives. He stopped running.
He stood still. He stared.

The lion opened his mouth wider—
so wide that Jack Tall could see his throat,
opened wide and deep and dark like
a tunnel to go into. Jack Tall went pale.

pale: to lose color
from the face due
to fear

16

Then the lion roared.

He ROARED and he ROARED and he **ROARED.**

All the teachers came running out.

All the children stopped playing and stuck their fingers in their ears. And the biggest boy, Jack Tall, turned around and ran and ran and ran. He never stopped running until he got home to his mother.

The little girl came out from behind the lion. "Well," she said, "I don't think much of *him*. I shall never be scared of *him* again."

"I was hungry," said the lion,
"I could easily have eaten him. Only I'd
promised you."

"And his mother wouldn't have liked it,"
said the little girl. "Time for afternoon
school now."

"I'm not staying for afternoon school,"
said the lion.

"See you on Monday then," said the
little girl. But the lion did not answer.
He just walked off.

On Monday the lion did not come to
school. At playtime, in the playground,
the biggest boy came up to the little girl.

"Where's your friend that talks so
loudly?" he said.

"He's not here today," said the little girl.

"Might he come another day?" asked the biggest boy.

"He might," said the little girl. "He easily might. So you just watch out, Jack Tall."

Why won't the little girl ever be afraid of Jack Tall again?

How does the lion help the little girl stand up to Jack Tall?

Why does the lion only roar at Jack Tall?

Why is Jack Tall the only one to run away from the lion?

Why does the little girl tell Jack Tall that the lion might come back?

Back on the Playground

I would like to take the lion _____

My Question

_____

_____

_____

Name _____

COYOTE RIDES THE SUN

NATIVE AMERICAN FOLKTALE

AS TOLD BY

JANE LOUISE CURRY

SESSION 1

INTRODUCTION

Begin the session by telling children that this is a Native American tale about a coyote who goes for a ride on the sun. Explain that a *coyote* is a small wolflike animal that lives on the *prairies*, flat, grassy lands in the western part of North America. You might want to orient children to the story by explaining that Coyote is a clever and tricky character who appears in many Native American tales.

FIRST READING AND SHARING OF RESPONSES

Ask children to listen as you read the story aloud. When you first come to the words "deeds," "falcon," "haunches," and "singed," explain them briefly, using the definitions given in the margin of your text.

After the reading, allow a few moments to clear up unfamiliar vocabulary and to let students ask questions and share their initial reactions to the story. Encourage children to offer their opinions about which parts of the story they especially liked and why.

ART ACTIVITY

Have children turn to the frontispiece, captioned "Coyote Rides the Sun." Tell them that they are going to draw a picture of Coyote when he rides the Sun. Help students get ideas for their pictures by having them think briefly about such things as how Coyote would feel being so high up in the sky on the hot, hot Sun and how Sun would look. Remind them that Sun is a character in the story who would have a face and a personality.

Allow time for students to share and compare their drawings.

SESSION 2

POSTING "MY QUESTIONS"

Have students cut out the questions they wrote at home and pin them on the Sharing Questions bulletin board. Children who have not had an at-home reading can dictate their questions to you at this time. Encourage children to look at the Sharing Questions bulletin board during the week, to point out their own questions and to ask about those of their classmates.

READING AND REVIEW OF G.B.'S QUESTIONS

Read the story aloud, encouraging children to follow along in their books if they can. Pause to collect students' responses to G.B.'s questions (pages 27, 33, and 39). Help students think further about their responses by asking follow-up questions such as those given in the margin of your text.

SESSION 2 (continued)

ART ACTIVITY

Have students turn to the page with the heading "Why is Coyote able to ride the Sun?" Read the question and tell students that the four reasons given are all good ones, and that they are going to discuss each one. Go through the reasons, asking children to explain how important they think each one is in helping Coyote achieve his goal. After the discussion, ask children to choose their favorite answer and illustrate it. As students draw, circulate among them and help them circle their answers. If children wish to choose and illustrate an answer not listed, help them write their answer in their books.

Allow time for children to share and compare their drawings.

SESSION 3

SHARING QUESTIONS DISCUSSION

Prepare for discussion as usual, deciding on the five or six interpretive questions you intend to ask the class. Note which of the children's questions are similar to those you plan to lead and try to include three or four of their questions in your final list. When you write your questions on the board, include children's names as appropriate.

Suggested Interpretive Questions

Why isn't Coyote proud and happy that he managed to ride the Sun? Has Coyote learned anything from riding the Sun?

Why does Coyote still think he will be able to ride the Sun and become chief of the animal people after he has failed twice to catch the Sun?

Why does Coyote think the animal people should serve him and bring him gifts when he is chief?

Why does Sun say he cannot shine more gently when Coyote begs him to do so? Is he trying to teach Coyote a lesson?

GROUP CREATIVE WRITING

Write on the board or a piece of chart paper the title "Early Morning Song" and the lines "Awake in the hour before dawn,/Awake in the hour before dawn." Read the title aloud to the class and remind them that, in the story, Coyote wants to get up early enough to catch the Sun. So, before he goes to bed, he sings to himself, "Awake in the hour before dawn, awake in the hour before dawn."

Tell students that they are going to write a song about times when *they* want to get up very early in the morning to do something special. Elicit students' ideas by asking them *When was a time **you** wanted to get up especially early? Why did you need to get up early in order to do this thing?* If students have difficulty remembering specific occasions, have them think of times a person *might* want to get up extra early. Record students' contributions on the blackboard or chart paper, beginning each line with "So I can…."

SESSION 3 (continued)

When the poem is finished, read it back to the class. Make copies for students to paste into their books on the page titled "Early Morning Song," or help them copy their favorite line in the space provided. If there is time, students can use the remaining space on the page to illustrate their favorite line.

Here is a brief example of a song that a class might compose:

Early Morning Song

Awake in the hour before dawn,
Awake in the hour before dawn,
So I can get to the lake to go fishing,
So I can get ready to go visit my grandparents,
So I can see the sun come up,
Awake in the hour before dawn.

SESSION 4

DRAMATIZATION AND EVALUATIVE DISCUSSION

Ask children to imagine that they are the animal people who live in Coyote's village. Tell them they are going to have a village meeting to decide whether or not they want to make Coyote their chief. Remind them of animals that are mentioned in the story, such as Prairie Falcon, Eagle, Bear, Wolf, and Badger, and suggest other animals that might also live in the village. Then give children a moment to decide what kind of animal person they want to be.

Begin the village meeting by writing on the board or chart paper the following question and headings:

Do you want Coyote to be chief of the animal people?

Yes   No

As children offer their opinions, ask for their reasons supported by the story, and write a word or two for each under the appropriate heading. Children may give reasons for both answers if they like.

After the class has debated the question for five or ten minutes, tell them that they are now going to vote for or against making Coyote their chief. Before the vote, briefly review all the reasons children have offered for both sides.

Once the students have voted, have them turn to the page with the question "Do you want Coyote to be chief of the animal people?" Reread the question and ask them to circle either "yes" or "no," depending on how they voted.

Circulate among children and help them circle their answers. If they like, children can also record their main reason for voting as they did on the lines provided.

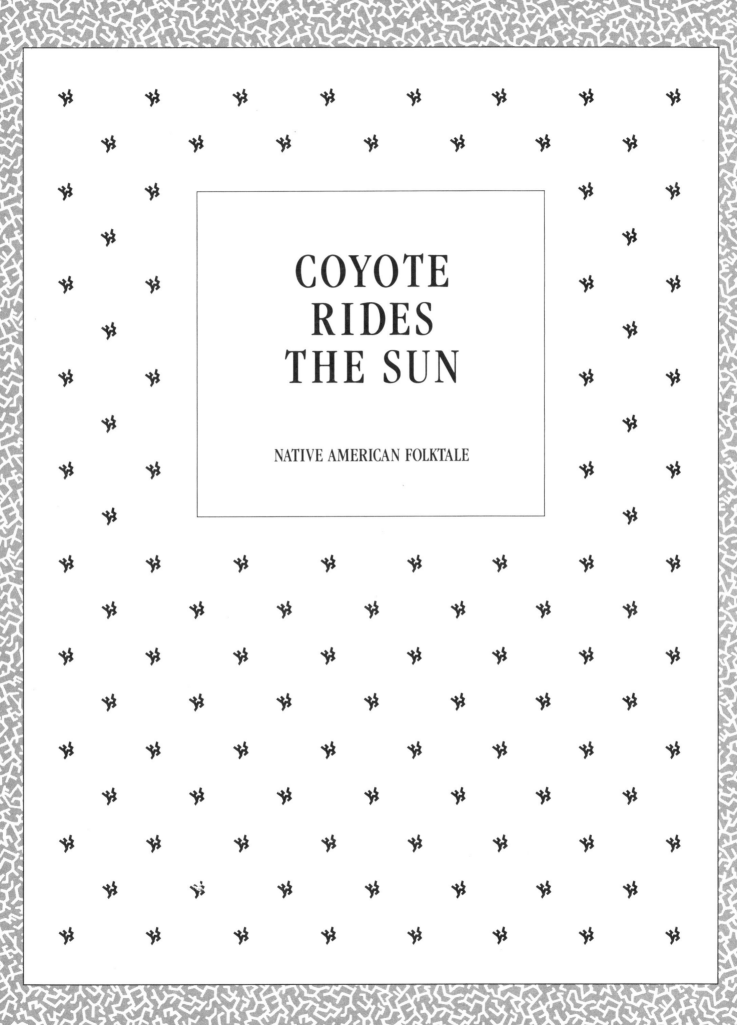

COYOTE
RIDES
THE SUN

NATIVE AMERICAN FOLKTALE

Coyote Rides the Sun

One day at sunset, back in the Beforetime, Coyote lay in the doorway to his house, and felt sorry for himself. "It is not fair," said he aloud to the clouds and sky. "What animal is as clever as I? Who has helped his people as much as I? Who has done more great deeds? The animal people should make me their chief, but they do not. Some even hide in their houses when they see me coming. How am I to show them how great I am?"

deeds: brave acts

Why does Coyote want to be chief of the animal people?

Why isn't the clever Coyote already chief of the animal people?

Why do some of the animals hide in their houses when they see Coyote coming?

Why does Coyote think that riding the Sun will show everyone how great he is?

falcon: a swift-flying bird that hunts

Just then, Sun rolled out of sight on his way down through the hole at the west end of the sky. Coyote, seeing this, sat up. He grinned.

"Hai, I have it! I shall ride the Sun across the sky! Everyone in the world will see me, and I shall be famous indeed. But—," he frowned. "Where can I climb up to Sun's road? Perhaps Prairie Falcon will know."

Early the next morning Coyote went to Prairie Falcon's house. "Friend Falcon," said he. "Tell me how to get to Sun's road from here."

"**Oh, that is easy**," Prairie Falcon replied. "It is only a short hop from the top of the Easternmost Mountain. You cannot miss it from there." And he showed him the road.

Coyote set off at a trot. But at
midmorning, just as he reached the foot
of the Easternmost Mountain, Sun looked
over the mountaintop, and soon was
hurrying westward across the sky.

"**Stop!**" called Coyote as he turned
back toward the plain. "**Stop, Sun, and
hear me!**"

But Sun rolled on without a word.

Coyote followed, shouting up to
the Sun, but he got no answer. At last,
as the afternoon shadows grew long,
he found himself back where he started.
Tired as he was, he went straight to
Prairie Falcon's house, and told him what
had happened.

"I am not so swift as you, friend Falcon," said Coyote. "When must I leave my house to reach the mountaintop on time?"

"**Oh, that is easy**," Prairie Falcon replied. "You must leave in the hour before dawn." And he showed him a shorter road to the mountain.

After his evening meal, Coyote went early to bed and sang to himself, *Awake in the hour before dawn, awake in the hour before dawn.* As he slipped into sleep, the song sang itself in his dream. *Awake in the hour before dawn.*

And he did. In the hour before dawn he took up his bow and his quiver of arrows and set out toward the east and the Easternmost Mountain. When he came to the mountaintop, he saw the Sun's road overhead. Looking out toward the eastern edge of the World, Coyote saw the Sun climb up into the sky.

"Hai!" said Coyote. "I will catch him this time." He crouched low to leap up onto the sky-road.

And landed in a heap on the ground.

"Hai! It is higher than it looks," said he to himself. "But I can reach it easily before Sun comes."

On his second try Coyote drew back a little distance and took a running jump… and again fell back to earth with a bump.

Coyote growled. "A short hop,"
Falcon had called it. But then Falcon had
wings.

As the Sun drew nearer and nearer,
Coyote gathered himself for one last leap.
He hunkered down on his haunches
and sprang up with all of his strength.
But he fell, as before, back onto the
mountaintop.

And Sun passed overhead, rolling
away to the west.

"**Stop!**" howled Coyote as he scrambled
down the mountainside. "**Stop, Sun,
and hear me!**"

But Sun rolled on without a sign
that he had heard.

haunches: the hips
of an animal

Coyote followed, calling after him, but once more by late afternoon he found himself back where he started. If ever he was to catch the Sun, he saw, he must go all the way to the East Hole in the Sky at the eastern edge of the World. But how was he to find it? "I will ask Prairie Falcon," Coyote decided. "He will know."

And so, tired as he was, Coyote went to Prairie Falcon's house and told him all that had happened. "Friend Falcon," said he, "how can I find the East Hole in the Sky?"

"**Oh, that is easy**," Prairie Falcon replied, and he told him of the road on the far side of the mountains that led through the desert to that very place.

Is Prairie Falcon being a friend to Coyote, or is he making fun of him?

Why does the clever Coyote keep going back to Prairie Falcon for advice?

Why doesn't Prairie Falcon ever tell Coyote how dangerous and uncomfortable riding the Sun would be?

Why does Prairie Falcon keep telling Coyote the things he wants to do are "easy"?

At dusk Coyote did not go hunting for his evening meal. Instead he went early to bed so that he could rise at middle-night for the journey to the hole in the sky. But he could not sleep. He saw himself astride the Sun, riding above the plains while all the animal people stared in wonder. He saw himself as chief, in Eagle's house. He saw Badger bringing him sacks of squirrels, Wolf coming with a pack full of pine nuts. He saw Bear come, bearing a big haunch of deer meat, and birds flocking to him with pele seeds and a fine feather cloak. The excitement was too much to bear. Coyote jumped up from his blankets, took up his bow and quiver of arrows, and raced off to the east by starlight. Better by far to be early than late!

Coyote ran all night, and came
before dawn to the hole in the sky at the
eastern edge of the World. There he sat
himself down at the very edge, his back to
the hole, so that Sun could not come out.
And he waited.

Before very long Sun came along.
From below the earth he looked up
and saw Coyote sitting there.

"Hai!" cried Sun. "Out of my way!
Move out of my way so the day may
dawn."

But Coyote did not move, and said
not a word.

"Ho!" called the Sun. "Move away.
I must not be late!"

But Coyote sat still, and made no
sign that he had heard.

singed: burned a little bit

So the Sun shone fiercely up at
Coyote, and Coyote grew hotter and
hotter. He curled his tail up under him,
but the tip stuck out and Sun singed it
with his heat. Sun shone angrily on
Coyote's back. As he grew hotter and
hotter, Coyote spat on his paws and
reached back to dampen down his coat.

"Hai!" exclaimed Sun at last. "*Why* do
you sit in my way to make me late,
Coyote?"

"I wish," said Coyote quickly—
for he feared he would soon be roasted—
"to ride you across the sky."

"Silly fellow!" said Sun. "No, never."

"Then I will not move," said Coyote. And he sat tight, though he could smell the hair on his back and the tip of his tail as Sun singed it.

"I am late! I am late!" Sun fretted. And at last he agreed, and Coyote jumped upon his back. He closed his eyes against Sun's brightness, taking a look only now and again as Sun climbed up the trail to the sky. The first part was steep and had steps like a ladder, but as the trail grew easier, Sun hurried to make up the time he had lost. As he hurried, he grew hotter and hotter.

And so did Coyote.

"Ho, I am thirsty!" croaked he. "Give me a drink of water."

"Tso!" snorted the Sun, but he slowed and gave him an acorn-cup full.

Coyote grew hotter and still more hot. His coat began to smoke. He saw the clear blue of Clear Lake below and longed to jump down from the sky, but the Sun was too high. By midday the light was almost brighter than Coyote could bear, and he cried out to Sun to shine more gently.

"I cannot," declared Sun.

In a little while Coyote opened his eyes to see how far they had traveled, then shut them quickly again. A little later he took another quick look. And another.

And this he kept up all afternoon to see how much closer they had come to earth. When at last Sun passed over the western mountains, Coyote jumped into the branches of a tall redwood tree, and clambered down into the cool forest shade.

"**Never again! No, never!**" said he.

And that is why Coyote's back and the tip of his tail are dark, and why he does not come out at noonday, but hunts at dawn and dusk.

Why does Coyote insist on riding the Sun when just sitting next to it singes his fur?

Why does Coyote not go out at noonday after his adventure with the Sun? Is he afraid of the Sun, or ashamed to be seen?

Does riding the Sun show that Coyote would be a good chief of the animal people?

Is Coyote brave or foolish to ride the Sun? (Circle your answer.)

BRAVE

FOOLISH

Why?

39

Why is Coyote able to ride the Sun? (Circle your favorite answer.)

1. He never gives up trying to catch the Sun.

2. He asks Prairie Falcon for help.

3. He tricks the Sun by blocking its hole.

4. He wants so badly to be chief of the animal people.

Early Morning Song

Awake in the hour before dawn,

Awake in the hour before dawn,

So I can _____

_____

Awake in the hour before dawn.

"Do you want Coyote to be chief of the animal people?"

YES   NO

_____

_____

My Question

_____

_____

Name _____

SEASONS

POETRY BY
NIKKI GIOVANNI,
ROBERT LOUIS STEVENSON,
AND
LANGSTON HUGHES

O V E R V I E W

SESSION 1: "Knoxville, Tennessee"

This session consists of an introduction, two readings of the poem, and an art activity in which children draw a picture showing what they like best about summer.

AT-HOME WORK: "Knoxville, Tennessee"

The adult partner reads the poem through once. The adult then reads the poem a second time, pausing to discuss G.B.'s two questions. Children respond to the first question by circling a part of the poem.

After reading, the adult writes the child's own question about "Knoxville, Tennessee" into the book.

SESSION 2: "Knoxville, Tennessee"

During this reading of the poem, you will collect students' responses to G.B.'s questions and lead a discussion of them. The session concludes with a group creative-writing activity in which children compose a poem about a favorite season in their hometown.

SESSION 3: "Picture-Books in Winter"

This session consists of an introduction and first reading of the poem, a second reading with textual analysis, and an art activity in which children draw a picture showing what they like most about their favorite story-book.

SESSION 4: "April Rain Song"

This session consists of an introduction and first reading of the poem, a second reading with textual analysis, and an art activity in which children draw a picture of something they enjoy doing when it is raining.

SESSION 1: "Knoxville, Tennessee"

INTRODUCTION

Introduce the poem by telling children that it is about summertime in the South, in a place called Knoxville, Tennessee.

FIRST AND SECOND READINGS

Ask children to listen as you read the poem aloud. Before reading the poem a second time, take a few moments to let children ask questions and make comments. Also help children clear up such unfamiliar vocabulary as "okra" and "gospel music," using the definitions given in the margin of your text.

Read the poem aloud a second time, encouraging students to follow along in their books if they can.

ART ACTIVITY

Have students turn to the page captioned "What I Like Best About Summer" and tell them that they are going to draw a picture showing what *they* especially like about the summertime.

Allow time for students to share and compare their drawings.

SESSION 2: "Knoxville, Tennessee"

POSTING "MY QUESTIONS"

Have students cut out the questions they wrote at home. Glance through them briefly and note any that you might want to raise during your discussion of G.B.'s questions. Then pin students' questions on the Sharing Questions bulletin board. Let children know that even though there will be no Sharing Questions Discussion this week, they should still look at the bulletin board and talk about their questions with each other.

READING AND REVIEW OF G.B.'S QUESTIONS

Read the poem aloud, pausing to collect students' responses to G.B.'s questions. Ask children to give reasons for their answers, and then help them think further about the poem by asking additional questions such as those given in the margin of your text.

GROUP CREATIVE WRITING

Tell children that they are going to write a poem about a season in their own hometown. On the board or a piece of chart paper, write the name of your town and state for the title of the poem, followed by the lines, "I always like _____ best/You can eat...."

SESSION 2: "Knoxville, Tennessee" (continued)

Complete the first line by having students choose their favorite season, or suggest that they might want to write about the present one. Help children begin thinking about why they like this season by having them list some things they particularly enjoy eating at this time of the year. After children have offered ideas about favorite foods, continue the poem in the same manner by adding new stanzas, one at a time, using such opening phrases as "You can go to," "You can listen to," "You can see," and "You can feel."

When the poem is finished, read it back to the class. Make copies for students to paste into their books, or help them copy their favorite lines in the space provided.

If time allows, children may use the remaining space on the page to illustrate their favorite lines.

Here is an example of a poem that a class might compose:

Chicago, Illinois

I always like autumn best
You can eat
turkey and pumpkin pie
taffy apples
and popcorn

You can go to
football games
Halloween parties
and the mall for new school clothes

You can see
pumpkins
brightly colored leaves
and birds flying south

SESSION 3: "Picture-Books in Winter"

INTRODUCTION

Introduce the poem by telling students that it is about how much fun it is to curl up and read picture-books in the wintertime.

FIRST READING

Ask children to listen as you read the poem aloud. Afterward, take a few moments to let children ask questions and make comments. Also help children clear up such unfamiliar vocabulary as "rook," "nurse," "put by," "crook," and "nursery nook," using the definitions given in the margin of your text.

SESSION 3: "Picture-Books in Winter" (continued)

SECOND READING AND TEXTUAL ANALYSIS

Read the poem through a second time, encouraging students to follow along in their books if they can, and to join in saying the underlined phrases. During this second reading, pause after the second, third, and last stanzas to conduct a textual analysis, using questions such as those printed in your text.

ART ACTIVITY

Have children turn to the page captioned "My favorite picture story-book is...." Tell children that they are going to think about *their* favorite story-book and draw a picture showing what they like best about it—for example, a special character or place, or an exciting event. Before they begin drawing, have children briefly exchange opinions about what their favorite books are and why they like them.

As children draw, circulate among them and help them complete their captions by writing in the title of their favorite story-book. Allow time for children to share and compare their pictures.

SESSION 4: "April Rain Song"

INTRODUCTION

Introduce the poem by telling children that it is about how nice rain can be in the springtime.

FIRST READING

Have children listen while you read the poem through once. Afterward, take a few moments to let children ask questions and make comments. Also help children clear up such unfamiliar vocabulary as "gutter," using the definition given in the margin of your text.

SECOND READING AND TEXTUAL ANALYSIS

Read the poem a second time, encouraging children to follow along in their books if they can, and to join in saying the underlined phrases.

After this second reading, conduct a textual analysis, using questions such as those printed in your text.

ART ACTIVITY

Have children turn to the page captioned "I love the rain because...." Tell children that they are going to draw a picture showing what they like to do the most when it is raining. Help children get ideas for their pictures by asking such questions as *Would you like to do something outside or stay inside? Why do you especially like to do this thing when it is raining?*

As children draw, circulate among them and help them complete their captions. Allow time for children to share and compare their pictures.

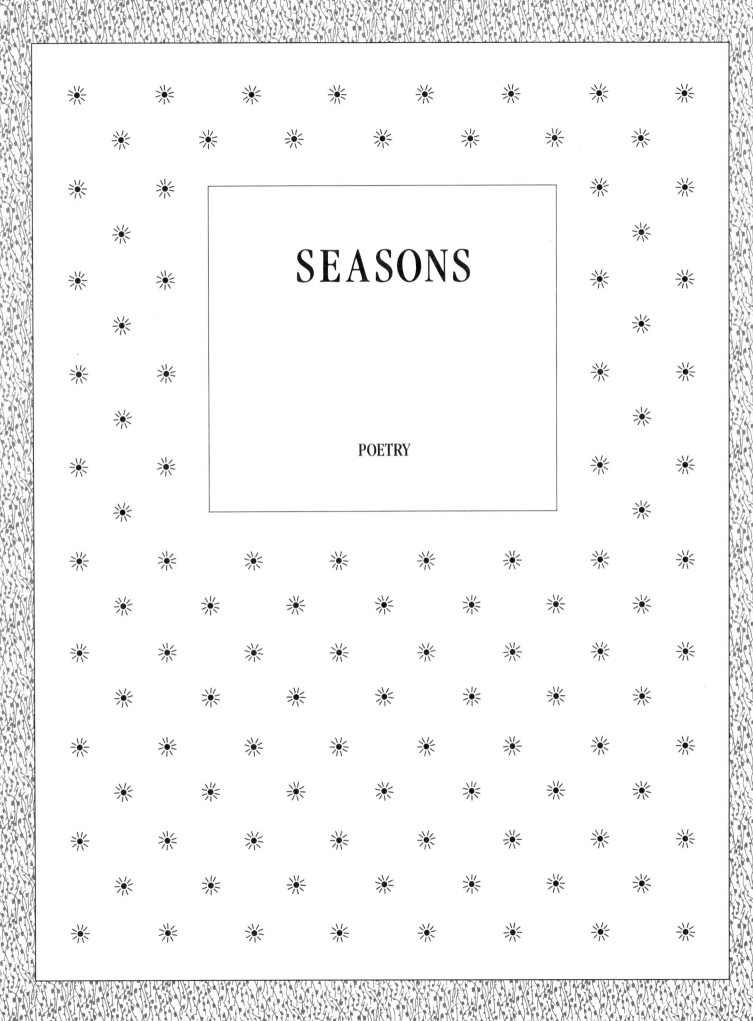

SEASONS

POETRY

KNOXVILLE, TENNESSEE

I always like summer
best
you can eat fresh corn
from daddy's garden
and okra
and greens
and cabbage
and lots of
barbecue
and buttermilk
and homemade ice-cream
at the church picnic

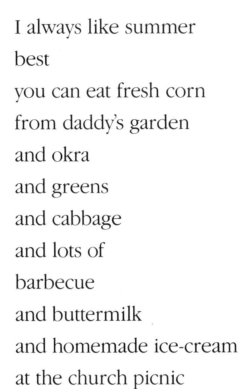

okra: a vegetable used in Southern cooking

Which of these summer foods would you most like to eat? (Circle your answer in the poem.)

Why would it be nice to eat food that you grew in your own garden?

Why does food seem to taste better at a picnic?

and listen to
gospel music
outside
at the church
homecoming
and go to the mountains with
your grandmother
and go barefooted
and be warm
all the time
not only when you go to bed
and sleep

—Nikki Giovanni

gospel music:
church songs that
originated in the
South

What kinds of
feelings do you
think the speaker
has about summer?

*Why is it fun to do
things with other
people in your
community?*

*What is so nice
about being able
to go barefooted?*

*Why does the
speaker like
feeling warm all
the time?*

What I Like Best About Summer

_____ , _____

(Your city)   (Your state)

I always like _____ best

You can eat _____

_____

_____

You can _____

_____

_____

49

My Question

Name

PICTURE-BOOKS
IN WINTER

Summer fading, winter comes—
Frosty mornings, tingling thumbs,
Window robins, winter rooks,
And the picture story-books.

rook: a bird
similar to a crow

Water now is turned to stone
Nurse and I can walk upon;
Still we find the flowing brooks
In the picture story-books.

All the pretty things put by,
Wait upon the children's eye,
Sheep and shepherds, trees and crooks,
In the picture story-books.

nurse: a woman whose job is to take care of children

put by: put away for a while (the sense of this stanza is that things that aren't present in reality are always available to children through the words and pictures in story-books)

crook: a shepherd's hooked walking stick

We may see how all things are,
Seas and cities, near and far,
And the flying fairies' looks,
In the picture story-books.

How am I to sing your praise,
Happy chimney-corner days,
Sitting safe in nursery nooks,
Reading picture story-books?

—Robert Louis Stevenson

nursery nook: a cozy spot in a child's bedroom or playroom

Textual Analysis Question

Why is reading picture story-books especially nice in winter?

My favorite picture story-book is _____

_____

APRIL RAIN SONG

Let the rain kiss you.
Let the rain beat upon your head with silver
    liquid drops.
Let the rain sing you a lullaby.

The rain makes still pools on the sidewalk.
The rain makes running pools in the gutter.
The rain plays a little sleep-song on
    our roof at night—

And I love the rain.

—Langston Hughes

gutter: a ditch along the side of a street that carries off water

Textual Analysis Questions

How can the rain kiss you?

How can rain sound like a lullaby?

Why does the speaker love the rain?

I love the rain because _____

_____

A NOTE ABOUT THE READ-ALOUD SELECTIONS

The stories and poems in the Read-Aloud program are of the same high quality as all Junior Great Books selections. To ensure that selections will repay the sustained attention they receive in the program, and will hold children's interest for an extended period of time, all have passed through a stringent and lengthy review process.

First and foremost, selections in the Read-Aloud program must be emotionally compelling and imaginatively engaging. In order for children to develop a love of reading, they must be exposed to literature that speaks to their feelings and experience. Stories that strike a profound chord in children help them learn that reading is more than a basic processing of information; it is an inexhaustible source of pleasure and insight.

The Read-Aloud selections must also be well-written, conveying to children the delights of the written word. Through vivid language and strong, evocative images, children can have fun with reading. They soon discover that words contain meaning and associations that can be explored, played with, and savored.

Finally, selections are tested to ensure they embody interpretive ideas and themes that both children and adults find meaningful. When works are rich in meaning, children feel their efforts to read and understand them are rewarded. As children work with the stories and poems, they develop confidence in their own perceptions, and they become motivated to learn to read for themselves. Moreover, selections that have as much meaning for adults as for children help ensure that Shared Inquiry will be a collaborative effort among teachers, parents, and children.

Like the Junior Great Books program for older students, the Read-Aloud program features literature from a variety of cultures, including Native American, Caribbean, Asian, European, and African. Each selection embodies universal themes that all children can readily embrace—themes such as fairness, friendship, growing up, and learning about people and nature. By pursuing these themes with classmates in the Shared Inquiry environment, children gain experience in exploring their own unique perspectives and enlarging their understanding of ideas common to the human experience.

THE JUNIOR GREAT BOOKS READ-ALOUD SERIES

DRAGON SERIES

Volume 1

The Frog Prince
Brothers Grimm as told by Wanda Gág

Guinea Fowl and Rabbit Get Justice
African folktale as told by Harold Courlander
and George Herzog

"Nature Speaks"
Poetry by Carl Sandburg, James Reeves,
and Federico García Lorca

Volume 2

Feraj and the Magic Lute
Arabian folktale as told by Jean Russell Larson

The Tale of Johnny Town-Mouse
Beatrix Potter

"Companions"
Poetry by A. A. Milne, Gwendolyn Brooks,
and Robert Louis Stevenson

Volume 3

Buya Marries the Tortoise
African folktale as told by W. F. P. Burton

The Huckabuck Family and How They Raised Pop
Corn in Nebraska and Quit and Came Back
Carl Sandburg

"Magical Places"
Poetry by Byrd Baylor, William Shakespeare,
and Martin Brennan

SAILING SHIP SERIES

Volume 1

The Shoemaker and the Elves
Brothers Grimm as told by Wanda Gág

The Frog Went A-Traveling
Russian folktale as told by Vsevolod Garshin

"Night into Dawn"
Poetry by Robert Hillyer and John Ciardi,
and a Mescalero Apache song

Volume 2

The Tale of Two Bad Mice
Beatrix Potter

Bouki Cuts Wood
Haitian folktale as told by Harold Courlander

"Fantasy"
Poetry by Sylvia Plath, Edward Lear,
and Lewis Carroll

Volume 3

Lion at School
Philippa Pearce

Coyote Rides the Sun
Native American folktale as told by
Jane Louise Curry

"Seasons"
Poetry by Nikki Giovanni, Langston Hughes,
and Robert Louis Stevenson

THE JUNIOR GREAT BOOKS READ-ALOUD SERIES

SUN SERIES

Volume 1

The Black Hen's Egg
French folktale as told by
Natalie Savage Carlson

The Mouse and the Wizard
Hindu fable as told by Lucia Turnbull

"Imagination"
Poetry by Leslie Norris, Mark Van Doren,
and Robert Louis Stevenson

Volume 2

Rumpelstiltskin
Brothers Grimm, translated by Ralph Manheim

Eeyore Has a Birthday and Gets Two Presents
A. A. Milne

"When I Grow Up"
Poetry by Rabindranath Tagore and X. J. Kennedy,
and a Chippewa song

Volume 3

The King of the Frogs
African folktale as told by Humphrey Harman

Snow-White and the Seven Dwarfs
Brothers Grimm, translated by Randall Jarrell

"Mysterious Animals"
Poetry by T. S. Eliot, Jenifer Kelly,
and Robert Graves

PEGASUS SERIES

Volume 1

Chestnut Pudding
Iroquois folktale as told by John Bierhorst

The Pied Piper
English folktale as told by Joseph Jacobs

"Fanciful Animals"
Poetry by Edward Lear and A. A. Milne

Volume 2

The Mermaid Who Lost Her Comb
Scottish folktale as told by Winifred Finlay

Hansel and Gretel
Brothers Grimm, translated by Randall Jarrell

"Special Places"
Poetry by Gwendolyn Brooks and Robert Frost,
and a Navajo poem

Volume 3

Mother of the Waters
Haitian folktale as told by Diane Wolkstein

Zlateh the Goat
Isaac Bashevis Singer

"Secret Messages"
Poetry by Robert Louis Stevenson,
Barbara Juster Esbensen, and Emily Dickinson

SAMPLE LETTERS TO PARENTS
LETTER #1: To be sent home before the program begins

Dear Parents:

Our class will soon begin a new activity, an interpretive reading and discussion program called the Junior Great Books Read-Aloud program. Each week in this program, I will read an outstanding story or group of poems to the class and lead students in discussions, dramatizations, creative writing, and art projects. The program's structure offers children ongoing opportunities to develop their ideas about a challenging work of literature and to share those ideas with others.

The Read-Aloud program stresses the enjoyment of literature for its own sake, while at the same time it develops comprehension, interpretive thinking, and oral and written language skills. By listening to and reflecting on works that are rich in meaning, children feel that their efforts at understanding are rewarded, and they become more motivated to learn to read for themselves.

One evening a week, I will ask you to join in the program. Your child will bring home his or her book so that you can read aloud the selection for the week. Included in the book are a few questions for your child to answer as he or she thinks best. These questions (printed inside boxes and signaled by the character "G.B.") are open-ended questions that have no one "right" answer. Sometimes you will be asked to help your child underline or circle something on the page. But mostly you will be listening to your child talk about his or her answers. While relaxed and fun, this at-home work is important because it will form the basis of your child's work with the selection in class for the rest of the week.

At the end of the selection, there is a space for you to write down your child's own question about the story or poem. This question will be posted on a bulletin board with those of the rest of the class; these questions will then be shared and discussed during the week.

Our first at-home session will be _____. Please plan to set aside about one half-hour with your child on _____ evenings for the next _____ weeks. I'm sure you and your child will find the Junior Great Books Read-Aloud program an enjoyable and rewarding experience.

If you are interested in assisting me with the Read-Aloud program in the classroom, please contact me at the following number: _____. If you have had past experience leading a Junior Great Books group, or would like to take the special training course, you could help me conduct the activities, such as reading selections aloud to the children or leading Sharing Questions Discussions. I am also looking for parents who would like to prepare Read-Aloud bulletin boards, help students write captions during art activities, or assist in some other way. I would be happy to hear from you.

Sincerely,

LETTER #2: *To be sent home at the time of the first at-home reading*

Dear Parents:

Your child is bringing home his or her Read-Aloud book tonight. This book will be sent home on a regular basis for the rest of the term. The children will be using their books in class during the week, so please make sure your child brings the book back to school the very next day. The Read-Aloud books will be your child's to keep.

Your child can tell you which story or poem to read, since we read it in class today. As your child's at-home partner, you will read the selection aloud, ask G.B.'s questions (printed in the boxes), and write down your child's own question about the selection. The only other writing you are required to do is to help your child circle or underline on the page when the directions say to do so. (See the brief instructions at the front of your child's Read-Aloud book.) *Please note that the rest of the writing assignments and all of the drawing activities will be completed in class.*

The main thing to keep in mind as you read and talk with your child is to enjoy yourselves! This is an opportunity for your child to talk and ask questions about the selection in an intimate setting. Remember that these questions have no single right answer, and that this is just the beginning of your child's work with the selection. Answers shouldn't be considered final. One way to help your child fully express his or her ideas is to follow up a statement by asking, "Why do you think this?" or, "Can you tell me more?"

Your curiosity about what your child is thinking and the example you set as a good listener will communicate a very important message about the value of discussing ideas and the importance of reading for meaning. The role you fill in the Read-Aloud program is a vital one.

Sincerely,

TEACHER'S PRESENTATION OF THE READ-ALOUD PROGRAM TO PARENTS

This semester I will be using an exciting reading and discussion program called the Junior Great Books Read-Aloud program. It may be new to you. I would like to tell you about it because I believe it will make a big difference in your child's attitude toward reading, and in the way he or she approaches problem solving in general.

The Junior Great Books Read-Aloud program is just what its name suggests. It is a program in which I will read aloud to your children challenging works of literature—folktales, modern children's classics, and distinguished children's poetry. You, too, will have a chance to read the selections aloud to your child and discuss them with him or her.

We have chosen to include this program in your children's curriculum because it will help them learn to ask questions and share answers about the *meaning* of a story or poem. Over the course of a week, the children will hear a selection read several times and will work with it through a variety of drawing, writing, and oral activities. The one element common to all of these activities is the sharing of ideas through discussion.

In this program, your children will exercise the whole range of oral and written language skills needed to become good readers. Because much of the Read-Aloud work is done in groups, the children will learn how to work together to unlock the rich meaning of good stories and poems. Equally important, they will acquire a sense of confidence about being able to figure out for themselves what at first seems puzzling or too difficult. We expect that these attitudes will carry over to their other schoolwork. I look forward to seeing the children become better able to raise thoughtful questions and listen to others' ideas, whether the subject is science, social studies, math, or literature.

THE READ-ALOUD CLASSROOM ROUTINE

This is what the children's Read-Aloud books look like. [*Display a copy.*] As you can see, there are places throughout the book for the children to respond to each selection through drawing and writing activities. [*Point out some of the blank activity pages.*] When the children are finished working with the stories and poems in a book, the book is theirs to keep. As a permanent record of your child's unique interpretation of the stories and poems, each book will be something to share proudly with you.

Now that you have had a glimpse of the books used in the Read-Aloud program, I would like to review briefly what a typical week's work on a story, or small group of poems, will be like. By doing so, I'll also be able to give you a better idea of where you fit into the program.

The First Reading of the Story

Usually, we will spend an entire week on a single story or small group of poems. This unhurried pace will give all the children an opportunity to show their strengths and discover new ones. A typical week begins with my reading a story or poem aloud to the children, after which they complete an assigned drawing that allows them to record their early responses to the selection. For example, after listening to the first reading of "The Frog Prince," the children will be asked to illustrate the thing the Princess had to do with the frog that *they* would have found the hardest to do. They can choose among such tasks as picking up the frog and carrying him, sharing a meal with him, and letting him sleep under the pillow. In choosing what to illustrate, the children are visualizing the characters and setting of the story. And as they make their own decisions about what the hardest thing is, they are learning that their individual perspectives on the story are important.

The At-Home Session

The second reading of the selection, which takes place at home with you or another adult partner, comes next. When reading the story aloud, you will want to encourage your child to follow along when possible and to repeat or join in saying any underlined words or phrases. You will also pause during your reading to ask several open-ended questions printed in the margins of the book. As you will note [*hold up book and display an example*], these questions are "boxed," and they are always accompanied by the Read-Aloud mascot, "G.B." (Incidentally, G.B.'s initials come from the name of the program—*Great Books*.) When discussing G.B.'s questions, you will want to keep in mind that there is no one "right" answer. These questions will be discussed again in class, at which time your child will have a chance to offer his or her ideas and to listen and respond to the thoughts of others.

The important thing for you to remember is that answers should never be considered final. Because this at-home session is a time for cozy, one-on-one work, you should encourage your children to take their time when they express their ideas. Also, help clear up any misunderstandings they might have about the facts of the story. At the end of the session, you will write—or help your child write—his or her own question about the selection into the book. [*Display "My Question" space.*] The next day, all the children's questions will be posted on a bulletin board, to be shared and discussed throughout the rest of the week.

The Third Reading of the Story and Discussion of the At-Home Work

All of the remaining work on a selection is completed in class. (This includes filling in the rest of the blank spaces in the book designated for writing or drawing.) During our second in-class session, I will read the selection aloud for the third time and, as I mentioned before, the class will talk about their answers to the questions discussed at home the previous night. This in-class discussion gives the children another opportunity to add to, or revise, their thinking about the selection. This session usually ends with a dramatization or an art activity based on the issues explored in the children's at-home work.

The Remaining Sessions

The remaining two sessions include writing activities, a group discussion of the selection, and additional dramatizations and art activities. The group discussion of the selection is a very important activity. It is based on five or six thought-provoking questions I have about the selection, and it includes, whenever possible, questions that the children produced during their at-home session. For example, a discussion of "The Frog Prince" might be based on such questions as "Why must the Princess be playmates with the frog before the spell over him can be broken?" and "Why does the frog get more and more demanding and bossy in the story?"

THE DRAMATIZATION, ART, AND WRITING ACTIVITIES

All of the dramatization, art, and writing activities in the Read-Aloud program help the children think more deeply about a selection. Dramatizations can make it easier for students to take in details and get plots straight. But dramatizations also help students interpret a story, as they think about what a character is feeling or thinking and about why that character acts as he or she does. For example, in the dramatization activity for "The Shoemaker and the Elves," children improvise two scenes: one in which the elves come to the shoemaker's workshop and make shoes, and one in which the elves find their new clothes. As they decide on words and actions for the scenes, the children are also exploring the elves' relationship with the shoemaker. The children are then better prepared to discuss such interpretive questions as "Why are the elves 'puzzled' by the clothes when they first see them?" and "Why do the clothes make the elves so happy that they 'run around like wild'?"

The art activities your child completes in the Read-Aloud book will be a visual record of his or her interpretation of different aspects of each story or poem. When you first examine your child's book, you will probably be struck by the fact that there are few professional illustrations, and that those few are done in black and white. This design was chosen because your child will be the chief illustrator of the book. Your child's drawings will reflect his or her own ideas about what a character is like, what the mood of a story or poem is, or why something happens. For example, a drawing assignment for Lewis Carroll's fantasy poem "The Lobster Quadrille" is preceded by a discussion in which children share ideas about why the creatures in the poem behave the way they do. Afterward, the children are asked to draw their favorite dancing sea creature from the poem, using such details as clothing and facial expressions to show what kind of personality they think that creature has. Naturally, each child's picture will be different, reflecting his or her individual ideas about this character and, by extension, about the poem as a whole. Usually, the art activities will end with the children sharing their drawings with the class, so that they have a chance to explain why they made their pictures as they did.

There will be many opportunities for the children to write in the Read-Aloud program. The writing activities for a single selection come in a variety of forms. Some activities are completed independently, with the children dictating to me when necessary, while others are "written" orally as a group. Some compositions are very brief, such as the questions the children write during the at-home session and the captions that they write in class for their drawings. The children will also write or dictate answers to thought-provoking questions about a selection. Finally, there are the creative-writing activities, such as the "Elf Song" the class will complete for the unit on "The Shoemaker and the Elves." This activity asks children to extend the song the elves sing near the end of the story. The children will add lines saying what they think the elves will do now that they have fine clothes and don't have to work anymore. Scheduled at the end of the week's work on the story, this activity builds on the children's interpretations of the elves' personalities and their reasons for helping the shoemaker, while also giving children the opportunity to exercise their imaginations. Like most of the creative-writing projects in the Read-Aloud program, this activity provides a framework of lines and verbal cues to help children generate and organize their ideas.

CONCLUSION

As I have tried to indicate in this short talk, the benefits of the Read-Aloud program will, I believe, prove to be far-reaching. At the same time that your children are learning about oral and written language, they will be discovering the excitement and satisfaction of critical thinking.

As the adult partner for the at-home session, you will have an ideal opportunity to encourage your child in this all-important endeavor. Your active interest in what your child is thinking about a selection will communicate a vital message to him or her about the importance of discussing ideas and the value of reading.

If any of you are interested in assisting me with the Read-Aloud program in the classroom, please let me know. If you have past experience leading Junior Great Books groups, or would like to take the special training course, you might consider helping me conduct the activities, such as reading the selections aloud to the children or leading the group discussion of a story or poem. I am also looking for parents who would like to prepare Read-Aloud bulletin boards, help students writing captions during the art activities, or assist in some other way.

Suggested handouts:

Photocopies of Appendix A, "A Note About the Read-Aloud Selections"

Photocopies of samples of student work from completed Read-Aloud books (if available)

READINGS
AND TOPICS
FOR AN
INTEGRATED
CURRICULUM

The Shoemaker and the Elves

Literature

Illustrated editions of "The Shoemaker and the Elves":
  Illustrated by Adrienne Adams. Translated by Wayne Andrews.
     Scribner's, 1960.
  Retold and illustrated by Cynthia and William Birrer. Lothrop, 1983.

Illustrated editions of tales by Jacob and Wilhelm Grimm:
  About Wise Men and Simpletons: Twelve Tales from Grimm. Illustrated
     by Nonny Hogrogian. Translated by Elizabeth Shub. Macmillan, 1971.
  The Brothers Grimm: Popular Folk Tales. Illustrated by Michael Foreman.
     Translated by Brian Alderson. Gollancz, 1978.
  Grimm's Fairy Tales: Twenty Stories. Illustrated by Arthur Rackham.
     Viking, 1973.
  Household Stories by the Brothers Grimm. Illustrated by Walter Crane.
     Translated by Lucy Crane. Dover, 1963.
  More Tales from Grimm. Freely translated and illustrated by Wanda Gág.
     Coward, 1947.
  Rare Treasures from Grimm: Fifteen Little Known Tales. Illustrated by
     Erik Blegvad. Compiled and translated by Ralph Manheim. Doubleday,
     1981.
  Tales from Grimm. Freely translated and illustrated by Wanda Gág.
     Coward, 1936.

Books written and illustrated by Wanda Gág (selected bibliography):
  The ABC Bunny. Coward, 1933.
  The Funny Thing. Coward, 1929.
  Gone Is Gone; or, The Story of a Man Who Wanted to Do Housework.
     Coward, 1935.
  Millions of Cats. Coward, 1928.
  Nothing at All. Coward, 1941.
  Snippy and Snappy. Coward, 1931.
  Snow-White and the Seven Dwarfs. Coward, 1938.

Social Studies

How Shoes Are Made

How a Business Works (buying raw materials, making products and selling them, reinvesting profits)

Science

Tanning Leather

Math

How Big Are Your Feet? *(measure length and width)*

Doubling *(chart on the blackboard how the pairs of shoes increase from one to two to four, etc.)*

The Frog Went A-Traveling

Literature

Russian tales:

> Afanasyev, Alexander Nikolaevich. *Soldier and Tsar in the Forest: A Russian Tale.* Translated by Richard Lourie. Illustrated by Uri Shulevitz. Farrar, 1972.
>
> Crouch, Marcus. *Ivan: Stories of Old Russia.* Illustrated by Bob Dewar. Oxford University Press, 1989.
>
> Daniels, Guy, trans. *Foma the Terrible: A Russian Folktale.* Illustrated by Imero Gobbato. Delacorte, 1970.
>
> Downing, Charles. *Russian Tales and Legends.* Illustrated by Joan Kiddell-Monroe. Walck, 1957.

Ginsburg, Mirra, trans. and ed. *The Lazies: Tales of the Peoples of Russia.* Illustrated by Marian Parry. Macmillan, 1973.

Lewis, Patrick J. *The Tsar and the Amazing Cow.* Dial, 1988.

Morton, Miriam, ed. *A Harvest of Russian Children's Literature.* University of California Press, 1967.

Pushkin, Alexander. *The Tale of Czar Sultan.* Translated by Patricia Lowe. Illustrated by I. Bilibin. T. Crowell, 1975.

_____. *The Tale of the Golden Cockerel.* Translated by Alessandra Pellizone. Illustrated by I. Bilibin. T. Crowell, 1975.

Ransome, Arthur. *Old Peter's Russian Tales.* Illustrated by Dmitri Mitrokhim. Nelson, 1917, 1976.

_____, ad. *The Fool of the World and the Flying Ship: A Russian Tale.* Illustrated by Uri Shulevitz. Farrar, 1968.

Robbins, Ruth. *Baboushka and the Three Kings.* Illustrated by Nicolas Sidjakov. Parnassus, 1960.

Whitney, Thomas P., trans. *The Story of Prince Ivan, the Firebird, and the Gray Wolf.* Illustrated by Nonny Hogrogian. Scribner's, 1968.

Wyndham, Lee, comp. *Tales the People Tell in Russia.* Illustrated by Andrew Antal. Messner, 1970.

Social Studies

Different Types of Transportation

Different Forms of Air Travel (helicopters, gliders, blimps, balloons, propeller and jet planes, rockets)

Science

Ducks and Why They Migrate

Frogs and How They Live

Life in Swamps

Math

Counting the Months and the Seasons *(make a circle of the twelve months and mark off the four seasons)*

Distributing a Load *(have different numbers of children try lifting the same heavy object)*

"Night into Dawn"

Literature

Native American poetry:

Allen, Terry, ed. *The Whispering Wind.* Doubleday, 1972.

Baylor, Byrd. *A God on Every Mountain Top.* Illustrated by Carol Brown. Scribner's, 1981.

Bierhorst, John, ed. *In the Trail of the Wind.* Farrar, 1971.

————. *The Sacred Path: Spells, Prayers, and Power Songs of the American Indians.* Morrow, 1983.

Brandon, William, ed. *The Magic World: American Indian Songs and Poems.* Morrow, 1971.

Clymer, Theodore, ed. *Four Corners of the Sky: Poems, Chants, and Oratory.* Illustrated by Marc Brown. Little, 1975.

Houston, James, ed. *Songs of the Dream People.* Illustrated by the author. Atheneum, 1972.

Jones, Hettie, ed. *The Trees Stand Shining: Poetry of the North American Indians.* Illustrated by Robert Andrew Parker. Dial, 1971.

Sneve, Virginia Driving Hawk, ed. *Dancing Teepees: Poems of American Indian Youth.* Holiday, 1989.

Wetherill, Hilda Faunce. *Navajo Indian Poems.* Vantage, 1952.

Poetry by John Ciardi (selected bibliography):

Doodle Soup. Illustrated by Merle Nacht. Houghton, 1985.

Fast and Slow: Poems for Advanced Children of Beginning Parents. Houghton, 1975.

I Met a Man. Illustrated by Robert Osborn. Houghton, 1961.

The Reason for the Pelican. Illustrated by Madeleine Gekiere. Lippincott, 1959.

You Read to Me, I'll Read to You. Illustrated by Edward Gorey. Lippincott, 1962.

Lullabies and night poems:

Larrick, Nancy, comp. *When the Dark Comes Dancing.* Illustrated by John Wallner. Philomel, 1983.

Rumble, Adrian, comp. *Shadow Dance: Poems of the Night for Young People.* Illustrated by Rowena Allen. Cassell (U.K.), 1987.

See also:

Hillyer, Robert. *Poems for Music 1917-1947.* Knopf, 1947.

Social Studies

Canoes: How They Are Made and How They Move
Apache Ceremonies and Daily Life
Halloween Customs

Science

What Causes the Colors Seen at Dawn and Sunset
Rainbows: What They Are and Why They Occur
The Color Spectrum *(illustrate with rainbows and prisms)*
Nocturnal Creatures (bats, owls, cats)

Math

Word Problems *(based on the numbers and objects in "Lullaby")*
Telling Time (sunset, midnight, sunrise)

The Tale of Two Bad Mice

Literature

Tales by Beatrix Potter:
    The Complete Tales of Beatrix Potter. Warne, 1989.

Social Studies

Dolls, Dollhouses, and Doll Furniture from Around the World
Childhood in England in Victorian and Edwardian Times (life in the nursery)

Science

Mice and How They Live

Math

Shapes and Sizes *(a hands-on experience matching shapes and sizes—can this object go through this hole?)*

Bouki Cuts Wood

Literature

Books by Harold Courlander (selected bibliography):

The King's Drum and Other Stories. Illustrated by Enrico Arno. Harcourt, 1962.

Olode the Hunter and Other Nigerian Tales. Harcourt, 1968.

People of the Short Blue Corn: Tales and Legends of the Hopi Indians. Illustrated by Enrico Arno. Harcourt, 1970.

The Piece of Fire and Other Haitian Folktales. Harcourt, 1964.

Courlander, Harold, and Herzog, George. *The Cow-Tail Switch and Other West African Stories.* Illustrated by Madye Lee Chastain. Holt, 1947.

Courlander, Harold, and Prempeh, Albert. *The Hat-Shaking Dance and Other Tales from the Gold Coast.* Illustrated by Enrico Arno. Harcourt, 1957.

Caribbean literature:

Agard, John. *Say It Again, Granny! Twenty Poems from Caribbean Proverbs.* Illustrated by Susanna Gretz. Bodley Head, 1986.

Berry, James. *Spiderman Anancy.* Holt, 1988.

Sherlock, Philip. *Anansi, the Spider Man: Jamaican Folk Tales.* Illustrated by Marcia Brown. T. Crowell, 1954.

————. *The Iguana's Tail: Crick Crack Stories from the Caribbean.* T. Crowell, 1969.

————. *West Indian Folk Tales.* Oxford University Press, 1988.

Sherlock, Philip and Hilary. *Ears and Tails and Common Sense.* T. Crowell, 1974.

Wolkstein, Diane. *The Magic Orange Tree and Other Haitian Folktales.* Illustrated by Elsa Henriquez. Knopf, 1978.

Social Studies

Life in the Caribbean
Beasts of Burden Around the World

Science

Donkeys and How They Live
Why Does Your Stomach Growl When You're Hungry?

Math

Right and Left Turns *(sketch simple maps of trails)*
Word Problems *(based on donkeys eating avocados)*

"Fantasy"

Literature

Poetry by Edward Lear (selected bibliography):
  The Complete Nonsense of Edward Lear. Dover, n.d.
  The Jumblies. Illustrated by Edward Gorey. W. R. Scott, 1968.
  The Owl and the Pussy-Cat. Illustrated by William Pène du Bois.
    Doubleday, 1962.
  The Quangle Wangle's Hat. Illustrated by Helen Oxenbury. Watts, 1969.
  The Scroobious Pip. Completed by Ogden Nash. Illustrated by Nancy
    Ekholm Burkert. Harper, 1968.
  Whizz! Illustrated by Janina Domanska. Macmillan, 1973.

Illustrated editions of Lewis Carroll's *Alice's Adventures in Wonderland:*
  Illustrated by Anthony Browne. Knopf, 1988.
  Illustrated by David Hall. Simon & Schuster, 1986.
  Illustrated by Arthur Rackham. Watts, 1966.
  Illustrated by John Tenniel. Macmillan, 1963.
  See also:
  Ovenden, Graham, ed. *The Illustrators of Alice in Wonderland and
    Through the Looking Glass.* St. Martin's, 1972.

Illustrated editions of Lewis Carroll's poetry:

> *Poems of Lewis Carroll.* Compiled by Myra Cohn Livingston. Illustrated by John Tenniel and others. T. Crowell, 1973.
>
> *The Walrus and the Carpenter and Other Remarkable Rhymes.* Illustrated by Julian Doyle. Salem House, 1986.

Social Studies

Tasks Elephants Perform (carrying howdahs; raising circus tents; lifting and moving heavy objects, such as trees)

Set and Square Dances (including the quadrille)

Science

Submarines

Sea Creatures (lobsters, sea turtles, porpoises, snails)

Simple Mechanics (cranks, wheels, cogs, levers)

Birds and Birding *(identify some of the birds named in "The Bed Book")*

How Snow Can Keep You Warm (the principle behind North-Pole beds and igloos)

Math

Nearness and Farness *(demonstrate the concept of relative nearness and farness, as in "The further off from England the nearer is to France")*

Lion at School

Literature

Books by Philippa Pearce (selected bibliography):

    The Battle of Bubble and Squeak. Andre Deutsch, 1979.

    Beauty and the Beast. Illustrated by Alan Barrett. Longman (U.K.), 1972.

    The Elm Street Lot. Illustrated by Peter Rush. Puffin, 1980.

    Emily's Own Elephant. Illustrated by John Lawrence. Greenwillow, 1988.

    Lion at School and Other Stories. Greenwillow, 1986.

    The Squirrel Wife. Illustrated by Derek Collard. T. Crowell, 1972.

    Who's Afraid? and Other Strange Stories. Greenwillow, 1987.

Social Studies

The Lion as King of Beasts

The Lion as a Symbol of Strength and Royalty *(use illustrations)*

How British and American Grade Schools Differ

Science

Lions and How They Live

Carnivorous and Herbivorous Animals: What and How They Eat *(consider the lion's sharp teeth)*

Math

Telling Time *(use clock faces to show the times for recess, lunch, going home, etc.)*

Coyote Rides the Sun

Literature

Coyote tales:

Baker, Betty. *And Me, Coyote!* Illustrated by Maria Horvath. Macmillan, 1982.

Bierhorst, John. *Doctor Coyote: A Native American Aesop's Fables.* Illustrated by Wendy Watson. Macmillan, 1987.

Curry, Jane Louise. *Back in the Beforetime: Tales of the California Indians.* Illustrated by James Watts. Margaret K. McElderry Books, 1987.

Haviland, Virginia, ed. *North American Legends.* Illustrated by Ann Strugnell. Putnam, 1979.

Martin, Fran. *Nine Tales of Coyote.* Illustrated by Dorothy McEntee. Harper, 1950.

Social Studies

The Role of Chief in a Tribe

Native Americans of California

Science

Coyotes and How They Live

Falcons and How They Live

Why Is the Sun Hottest in the Middle of the Day?

Math

Temperature *(use a thermometer to measure and read temperatures)*

"Seasons"

Literature

Poetry by Nikki Giovanni (selected bibliography):

Ego-Tripping and Other Poems for Young People. Illustrated by George Ford. Lawrence Hill, 1974.

Spin a Soft Black Song, rev. ed. Illustrated by George Martins. Farrar, 1987.

Vacation Time: Poems for Children. Morrow, 1981.

Illustrated editions of Robert Louis Stevenson's *A Child's Garden of Verses:*

Illustrated by Jessie Willcox Smith. Scribner's, 1905, 1969.

Illustrated by Tasha Tudor. Walck, 1947.

Illustrated by Brian Wildsmith. Watts, 1966.

Poetry by Langston Hughes (selected bibliography):

Black Misery. Illustrated by Arouni. Eriksson, 1969.

Don't You Turn Back. Selected by Lee Bennett Hopkins. Illustrated by Ann Grifalconi. Knopf, 1969.

Fields of Wonder. Knopf, 1947.

Selected Poems of Langston Hughes. Knopf, 1959.

Social Studies

Gospel Music *(use recordings, if possible)*

Shepherding and Wool Production

Regional Foods of North America

Different Kinds of Gardens

How Books Are Made

Science

Freezing: How Water Becomes Ice

What Causes Rain

What Causes the Seasons to Change

Why Do Different Places Have Different Climates? *(compare the seasons in your area with those in other parts of the country)*

Math

Measuring Temperatures (freezing, boiling, room temperature at different times)

Measuring Quantities (rainfall, ingredients in recipes, amounts of food for a picnic)

Acknowledgments

All possible care has been taken to trace ownership and secure permission for each selection in this series. The Great Books Foundation wishes to thank the following authors, publishers, and representatives for permission to reprint copyrighted material:

The Shoemaker and the Elves, from TALES FROM GRIMM, by Jacob and Wilhelm Grimm, freely translated and illustrated by Wanda Gág. Copyright 1936 by Wanda Gág; renewed 1964 by Robert Janssen. Reprinted by permission of Coward, McCann & Geoghegan.

The Frog Went A-Traveling, by Vsevolod Garshin, from A HARVEST OF RUSSIAN CHILDREN'S LITERATURE, edited by Miriam Morton. Copyright 1967 by Miriam Morton. Reprinted by permission of Lewis Morton.

"Lullaby," from POEMS FOR MUSIC 1917-1947, by Robert Hillyer. Copyright 1947 by Robert Hillyer; renewed 1975 by Frances P. Hillyer and Elizabeth V. Hillyer. Reprinted by permission of Alfred A. Knopf, Inc.

"What Night Would It Be?" from YOU READ TO ME, I'LL READ TO YOU, by John Ciardi. Copyright 1962 by John Ciardi. Reprinted by permission of Harper & Row, Publishers, Inc.

Bouki Cuts Wood, from THE PIECE OF FIRE AND OTHER HAITIAN FOLKTALES, by Harold Courlander. Copyright 1964 by Harold Courlander. Reprinted by permission of the author.

THE BED BOOK by Sylvia Plath. Copyright 1976 by Ted Hughes. Reprinted by permission of Harper & Row, Publishers, Inc.

Lion at School, from LION AT SCHOOL AND OTHER STORIES, by Philippa Pearce. Copyright 1971, 1977, 1979, 1985 by Philippa Pearce. Reprinted by permission of Greenwillow Books, a division of William Morrow & Company, Inc.

Coyote Rides the Sun, from BACK IN THE BEFORETIME: TALES OF THE CALIFORNIA INDIANS, retold by Jane Louise Curry. Copyright 1987 by Jane Louise Curry. Reprinted by permission of Margaret K. McElderry Books, an imprint of Macmillan Publishing Company.

"Knoxville, Tennessee," from EGO-TRIPPING AND OTHER POEMS FOR YOUNG PEOPLE, by Nikki Giovanni. Copyright 1973 by Nikki Giovanni. Reprinted by permission of the author.

"April Rain Song," from THE DREAM KEEPER AND OTHER POEMS, by Langston Hughes. Copyright 1932 by Alfred A. Knopf, Inc.; renewed 1960 by Langston Hughes. Reprinted by permission of Alfred A. Knopf, Inc.